**DATE DUE**

| NOV 1 8 2002 | | | |
|---|---|---|---|
| | | | |
| | | | |
| | | | |
| | | | |
| | | | |
| | | | |
| | | | |
| | | | |
| | | | |
| | | | |
| | | | |
| | | | |
| | | | |
| | | | |
| | | | |

Demco

# THE
# BEAUTIFUL IN MUSIC

Da Capo Press Music Reprint Series

GENERAL EDITOR

ROLAND JACKSON

UNIVERSITY OF SOUTHERN CALIFORNIA

# THE
# BEAUTIFUL IN MUSIC

A Contribution to the Revisal of
Musical Aesthetics

by
## Eduard Hanslick

Translated from the Seventh Edition, Enlarged
and Revised (Leipzig, 1885)
by Gustav Cohen

DA CAPO PRESS • NEW YORK • 1974

Library of Congress Cataloging in Publication Data

Hanslick, Eduard, 1825-1904.
  The beautiful in music.

  (Da Capo Press music reprint series)
  Translation of Vom Musikalisch-Schönen.
  Reprint of the 1891 ed. published by Novello, London
New York.
  1. Music—Philosophy and aesthetics.  I.  Title.
ML3847.H3  1974              780'.1              74-1362
ISBN 0-306-70649-0

This edition of *The Beautiful in Music* is an unabridged republication of the first english language edition published in London and New York in 1891.

Published by Da Capo Press, Inc.
A Subsidiary of Plenum Publishing Corporation
227 West 17th Street, New York, N.Y. 10011

Manufactured in the United States of America

THE

# BEAUTIFUL IN MUSIC

A CONTRIBUTION TO

THE REVISAL OF MUSICAL ÆSTHETICS

BY

## DR. EDUARD HANSLICK

*Professor at the Vienna University.*

SEVENTH EDITION, ENLARGED AND REVISED (LEIPZIG, 1885),

TRANSLATED BY GUSTAV COHEN

*And dedicated to his Friends*

MR. AND MRS. F. COLLIER.

———

*LONDON & NEW YORK*

NOVELLO, EWER AND CO.

—

1891.

DEDICATED TO

# ROBERT ZIMMERMANN

PROFESSOR OF PHILOSOPHY AT THE VIENNA UNIVERSITY,

BY HIS FAITHFUL FRIEND

## THE AUTHOR.

# CONTENTS.

# TRANSLATOR'S PREFACE.

IF I have ventured to translate Dr. Eduard Hanslick's "Vom Musikalisch-Schönen," I have done so with a full knowledge of the shortcomings which every translation must present, and especially one like this, the original of which is so inimitable in style and so thoroughly German in construction, that even far more competent writers than myself would find it difficult, if not impossible, to do complete justice to it. My excuse for undertaking so arduous a task must be the desire to introduce to the English reader one of the most remarkable books on musical æsthetics, and one which has deservedly gained a wide reputation among the German-speaking communities. The work is not of recent date, the first edition having appeared close on forty years ago; yet, as is the case with all works dealing with principles and not with questions of local or contemporary interest, the fact of its age in no way detracts from its importance. In conclusion, I may say that I have not aimed so much at perfection in style as at reflecting with fidelity the mind and spirit of the author.

GUSTAV COHEN.

Sale, *May*, 1891.

# PREFACE TO THE SEVENTH EDITION.

THIS, the seventh edition of the work which first appeared in the year 1854, does not differ materially from the fifth (1876) and the sixth (1881) editions, but merely contains some explanatory and amplifying additions. By way of introducing it to the public I should best like to borrow the words with which the estimable Fr. Th. Vischer has just prefaced the reprint of an older essay of his ("Der Traum").[*]
"I include this essay," says Vischer, "in the present series, without shielding it from the attacks which have been levelled against it. I have also refrained from improving it by retouches, excepting a few unimportant alterations. I might now, perhaps, here and there choose a different mode of expression, give a fuller exposition, or assert things in a more qualified and guarded manner. Who is ever completely satisfied with a work which he reads again after the lapse of years? Yet we know but too well that corrective touches often rather spoil than improve."

If I were to enter upon a polemic campaign, and

---

[*] "Altes und Neues," von Fr. Th. Vischer (Stuttgart 1881), page 187.

reply to all criticisms which my book has provoked, this volume would grow to an alarming size.  My convictions have remained unaltered, and so has the irreconcilable antagonism of the contrary musical parties of the present day.* The reader will, therefore, no doubt, allow me to repeat some of the remarks which I made in the preface to the third edition.  I know the shortcomings of this essay but too well; still, the favourable reception accorded to the earlier editions—a reception which far exceeded my expectations—and the highly gratifying interest taken in the book by eminent experts, proficient both as philosophers and musicians, have convinced me that my views—the somewhat categorical and rhapsodical manner in which they were originally stated, notwithstanding—had fallen on fertile ground.  A very notable concurrence with these views I found, to my agreeable surprise, in the aphorisms and short essays on music by Grillparzer, published only some ten years ago, after the poet's death.  Some of the most valuable of his propositions I could not refrain from quoting in this new edition, while in my essay

---

* O. Hostinsky's interesting and carefully worded essay ("Das Musikalisch-Schöne und das Gesammtkunstwerk von Standpunkt der formalen Æsthetik," Leipzig, 1877) is a paradoxical exception. Though in the first part he, to all appearance, clearly and fully endorses my premises, he subsequently, on discussing the term "Kunstverein" (the combination of arts), narrows, twists, and interprets them in such a manner as to reach conclusions completely at variance with my own.

" Grillparzer und die Musik," I have discussed
them at greater length.*

Certain vehement opponents of mine have occa-
sionally imputed to me a flat and unqualified denial
of whatever goes under the name of feeling ; but
every dispassionate and attentive reader will have
readily observed that I only protest against the
intrusion of the feelings upon the province of
*science*, in other words—that I take up the cudgels
against those æsthetic enthusiasts who, though
presuming to teach the musician, in reality only
dilate upon their tinkling opium-dreams.  I am
quite at one with those who hold that the ultimate
worth of the beautiful must ever depend upon the
immediate verdict of the feelings.  But at the same
time I firmly adhere to the conviction, that all the
customary appeals to our emotional faculty can
never show the way to a single musical law.

This conviction forms one of the propositions—
*the principal but negative proposition*—of this enquiry
which is mainly and primarily directed against the
widely-accepted doctrine that the office of music is
" to represent feelings."  It is difficult to see why
this should be thought equivalent to " affirming that
music is absolutely destitute of feeling."  The rose
smells sweet, yet its subject is surely not the representation of the odour ; the forest is cool and shady,

---

* " Musikalische Stationen," by Ed. Hanslick (Berlin : published
by G. Hoffmann, 1878, page 331, &c.)

but it certainly does not *represent* "the feeling of coolness and shadiness." It is not a mere verbal quibble if the term "to represent" is here expressly taken exception to, for it is this term which is answerable for the grossest errors in musical æsthetics. The "representing" of something always involves the conception of two separate and distinct objects which by a special act are purposely brought into relation with each other.

Emanuel Geibel, by a felicitously chosen parallel, has described this relation in the following distich, with greater perspicuity and more agreeably than philosophic analyses could ever do :—

"Warum glückt es dir nie, Musik mit Worten zu schildern?
Weil sie, ein rein Element, Bild und Gedanken verschmäht.
Selbst das Gefühl ist nur wie ein sanft durchscheinender
Flussgrund,
Drauf ihr klingender Strom sinkend und schwellend entrollt."

Now, as I have reason to believe that the author of these beautiful lines was inspired by thoughts which this essay suggested, it appears to me that my views so vigorously denounced by romantic enthusiasts are, after all, quite compatible with true poetry.

The *negative* proposition referred to is complemented by its correlative, the *affirmative* proposition ; the beauty of a composition is *specifically musical—i.e.*, it inheres in the combinations of musical sounds and is independent of all alien, extra-musical notions. The author has honestly endeavoured to make an exhaustive enquiry into the positive aspects of the "musically beautiful," upon which the very existence of our art and the supreme laws of its æsthetics depend. If, nevertheless, the controversial and negative elements predominate, I must plead the circumstances of the time as my excuse. When I wrote this treatise, the advocates of the "music of the future" were loudest in their praises of it, and could but provoke a reaction on the part of people holding opinions such as I do. Just when I was busy preparing the second edition, "Liszt's Programme-Symphonies" had appeared, which denied to music more completely than ever before its independent sphere, and dosed the listener with it as a kind of vision-promoting medicine. Since then, the world has been enriched by Richard Wagner's "Tristan," "Nibelungen Ring," and his doctrine of the *infinite melody*—*i.e.*, formlessness exalted into a principle; the intoxicating effect of opium manifested both in vocal and instrumental music, for the worship of which a temple has been specially erected at Bayreuth.

I trust I may be pardoned, if in view of such symptoms I felt no inclination to abbreviate or temper the polemic part of this essay; but pointed, on the contrary, more emphatically than ever to the one and immutable factor in music, to *purely musical beauty*, such as our great masters have embodied in their works, and such as true musical genius will produce to the end of time.

EDUARD HANSLICK.

VIENNA, *January*, 1885.

# CHAPTER I.

THE course hitherto pursued in musical æsthetics has nearly always been hampered by the false assumption that the object was not so much to enquire into what is beautiful in music, as to describe the feelings which music awakens. This view entirely coincides with that of the older systems of æsthetics, which considered the beautiful solely in reference to the sensations aroused, and the philosophy of beauty as the offspring of sensation (αἴσθησις).

Such systems of æsthetics are not only unphilosophical, but they assume an almost sentimental character when applied to the most ethereal of all arts, and though no doubt pleasing to a certain class of enthusiasts, they afford but little enlightenment to a thoughtful student, who, in order to learn something about the real nature of music, will, above all, remain deaf to the fitful promptings of passion, and not, as most manuals on music direct, turn to the emotions as a source of knowledge.

The tendency in science to study, as far as possible, the objective aspect of things could not but affect researches into the nature of *beauty*. A satisfactory result, however, is only to be attained by relinquishing a method which starts from subjective

sensation, only to bring us face to face with it once
more, after taking us for a poetic ramble over the
surface of the subject. Any such investigation will
prove utterly futile, unless the method obtaining in
natural science be followed at least in the sense of
dealing with the things themselves, in order to
determine what is permanent and objective in them,
when dissociated from the ever-varying impressions
which they produce.

Poetry, sculpture, and painting are, in point of
well-grounded æsthetic treatment, far in advance of
music. Few writers on these subjects still labour
under the delusion that from a general metaphysical
conception of beauty (a conception which necessarily
varies with the art) the æsthetic principles of any
specific art can be deduced. Formerly, the æsthetic
principles of the various arts were supposed to be
governed by some supreme metaphysical principle of
general æsthetics. Now, however, the conviction is
daily growing that each individual art can be understood only by studying its technical limits and its
inherent nature. " Systems " are gradually being
supplanted by "researches," founded on the thesis
that the laws of beauty for each art are inseparably
associated with the individuality of the art, and the
nature of its medium.*

---

* Robert Schumann has done a great deal of mischief by his
proposition (Collected Works I., 43) :—" The æsthetic principles of
" one art are those of the others, the material alone being different."
Grillparzer expresses a very different opinion and takes the right
view when he says (Complete Works IX., 142) :—" Probably no worse
" service has ever been rendered to the arts than when German

In æsthetics of rhetoric, of sculpture, and painting, no less than in art-criticism—the practical application of the foregoing sciences—the rule has already been laid down that æsthetic investigations must, above all, consider the beautiful *object*, and not the perceiving *subject*.

*Music* alone is unable, apparently, to adopt this objective mode of procedure. Rigidly distinguishing between its theoretico-grammatical rules and its æsthetic researches, the former are generally stated in extremely dry and prosaic language, while the latter are wrapped in a cloud of high-flown sentimentality. The task of clearly realising music as a self-subsistent form of the beautiful, has hitherto presented unsurmountable difficulties to musical æsthetics, and the dictates of "emotion" still haunt their domain in broad daylight. Beauty in music is still as much as ever viewed only in connection with its subjective impressions, and books, critiques, and conversations continually remind us that *the emotions* are the only æsthetic foundation of music, and that they alone are warranted in defining its scope.

"writers included them all in the collective name of art. Many "points they undoubtedly have in common, yet they widely diverge "not only in the means they employ, but also in their fundamental "principles. The essential difference between music and poetry "might be brought into strong relief by showing that music primarily "affects the senses and, after rousing the emotions, reaches the "intellect last of all. Poetry, on the other hand, first raises up an "idea which in its turn excites the emotions, while it affects the "senses only as an extreme result of its highest or lowest form. "They, therefore, pursue an exactly opposite course, for one "spiritualises the material, whereas the other materialises the "spiritual."

Music, we are told, cannot, like poetry, entertain the mind with definite conceptions, nor yet the eye, like sculpture and painting, with visible forms. Hence, it is argued, its object must be to work on the *feelings*. " Music has to do with feelings." This expression " has to do" is highly characteristic of all works on musical æsthetics. But what the *nature* of the link is that connects music with the emotions, or certain pieces of music with certain emotions ; by what laws of nature it is governed, what the canons of art are that determine its form—all these questions are left in complete darkness by the very people who have "to do" with them. Only when one's eyes have become somewhat accustomed to this obscurity does it become manifest that the emotions play a double part in music, as currently understood.

On the one hand it is said that the *aim* and *object* of music is to excite emotions—*i.e.*, pleasurable emotions ; on the other hand, the emotions are said to be the *subject-matter* which musical works are intended to illustrate.

Both propositions are alike in this, that one is as false as the other.

The refutation of the first of these propositions, which forms the introduction to most manuals of music, must not detain us long. The beautiful, strictly speaking, *aims at nothing*, since it is nothing but a *form* which, though available for many purposes according to its *nature* has, as such, no aim beyond itself. If the contemplation of something beautiful arouses pleasurable feelings, this effect is distinct from the beautiful as such. I may, indeed, place a beautiful object before an observer, with the avowed purpose of giving him pleasure, but this purpose in no way affects the beauty of the object. The beautiful is and remains beautiful though it arouse no emotion whatever, and though there be no one to look at it. In other words, although the beautiful exists *for* the gratification of an observer, it is *independent* of him.

In this sense music, too, has no *aim* (object) and the mere fact that this particular art is so closely bound up with our feelings, by no means justifies the assumption that its æsthetic principles depend on this union.

In order to critically examine this relation, we must, in the first place, scrupulously distinguish between the terms "feeling" and "sensation," although in ordinary parlance no objection need be raised to their indiscriminate use.

*Sensation* is the act of perceiving some sensible quality, such as a sound or a colour, whereas *feeling* is the consciousness of some psychical activity—*i.e.,* a state of satisfaction or discomfort.

If I note (perceive) with my senses the odour or taste of some object, or its form, colour, or sound, I call this state of consciousness *my sensation* of these qualities; but if sadness, hope, cheerfulness or hatred appreciably raise me above, or depress me below the habitual level of mental activity, I am said to *feel.**

---

* Older philosophers agree with modern physiologists in the definition of these terms, and we unhesitatingly prefer this definition to the terminology of Hegel's school of philosophy, which, as is well known, distinguishes between internal and external sensations.

The beautiful, first of all, affects our senses. This, however, is not peculiar to the beautiful alone, but is common to all phenomena whatsoever. Sensation, the beginning and condition of all æsthetic enjoyment, is the source of *feeling* in its widest sense, and this fact presupposes some relation, and often a highly complex one, between the two. No art is required to produce a *sensation ;* a single sound or colour may suffice. As previously stated, the two terms are generally employed promiscuously ; but older writers speak of "sensation," where we should use the term "feeling." (What those writers intend to convey, therefore, is that the object of music is to arouse our *feelings,* and to fill our hearts with piety, love, joy, or sadness.)

(In point of fact, however, this is the aim neither of music nor of any other art. An art aims, above all, at producing something *beautiful* which affects not our feelings, but the organ of pure contemplation, our *imagination.**)

It is rather curious that musicians and the older writers on æsthetics take into account only the contrast of "feeling" and "intellect," quite oblivious of the fact that the main point at issue lies *half-way between* the horns of this supposed dilemma. A

---

* Hegel has shown that the method of examining into the "sensations" (*i.e.,* "feelings" according to our terminology) which a work of art awakens, proceeds on indefinite lines and ignores the truly concrete element altogether. "What we are sensible of," he says, "is indissolubly connected with the most abstract and individual "subjectivity. The several kinds of sensations produced are, therefore, "different in a subjective sense only and not distinct modes of the "thing itself." (*Æsthetik* I., 142.)

musical composition originates in the composer's imagination, and is intended for the imagination of the listener. Our imagination, it is true, does not merely *contemplate* the beautiful, but it contemplates it with *intelligence*, the object being, as it were, mentally inspected and criticised. Our judgment, however, is formed so rapidly, that we are unconscious of the separate acts involved in the process, whence the delusion arises that, what in reality depends upon a complex train of reasoning, is merely an *act of intuition*.

The word "Anschauung" (viewing, contemplating) is no longer applied to visual processes only, but also to the functions of the other senses. It is, in fact, eminently suited to describe the act of attentive hearing which is nothing but a mental inspection of a succession of musical images. Our imagination, withal, is not an isolated faculty, for though the vital spark originates in the senses, it forthwith kindles the flame of the intellect and the emotions. A true conception of the beautiful is, nevertheless, independent of this aspect of the question.

In the pure act of listening, we enjoy the music alone, and do not think of importing into it any extraneous matter. But the tendency to allow our feelings to be aroused, implies something extraneous to the music. An exclusive activity of the *intellect*, resulting from the contemplation of the beautiful, involves not an æsthetic, but a *logical* relation, while a predominant action on the feelings brings us on still more slippery ground, implying, as it does, a *pathological* relation.

These inferences, drawn long ago from principles of general æsthetics, apply with equal force to the beautiful in every art. (If *music*, therefore, is to be treated as an *art*, it is not our feelings, but our imagination which must supply the æsthetic tests.) It is as well to make this premise hypothetical, seeing that the soothing effect of music on the human passions is always affirmed with such emphasis, that we are often in doubt whether music is a police regulation, an educational rule, or a medical prescription.

Yet, musicians are less prone to believe that *all* arts must be uniformly gauged by our feelings, than that this principle is true of *music* alone. It is this very power and tendency of music to arouse in the listener any given emotion which, they think, distinguishes *this art* from all the others.*

As on a previous occasion we were unable to accept the doctrine that it is the aim of art in general to produce any such effect, we are now equally unable to regard it as the specific aim of *music* to do so. Grant that the true organ with which the beautiful is apprehended is the *imagination*, and it follows that *all* arts are likely to affect the feelings indirectly.

---

* At a time when no distinction was made even between " feeling" and "sensation," a more critical examination into the varieties of the former was, of course, out of the question. Sensuous and intellectual feelings, the enduring state known as *frame of mind*, the acute or *emotional* state, inclination and passion, no less than the gradations peculiar to the latter, the " pathos " of the Greeks and the " passio " of the more modern Romans, were all confounded in one inextricable jumble, while of music nothing was predicated, except that it was the art of exciting emotions.

Are we not moved by a great historical picture with
the vividness of actual experience ?   Do not
Raphael's Madonnas fill us with piety, and do not
Poussin's landscapes awaken in us an irresistible
desire to roam about in the world ?   Do our feelings
remain callous to a sight such as the Strasburg
Cathedral ?   All these questions admit of but one
reply, which is equally true of poetry and of many
extra-æsthetic states of mind, such as religious
fervour, eloquence, &c.   We thus see that all other
arts, too, affect us with considerable force.   The
inherent peculiarities assumed to distinguish music
from the other arts would depend, therefore, upon
the degree of intensity of this force. ⟮ The attempt,
however, thus to solve the problem, is not only
highly unscientific, but is, moreover, of no avail,
because the decision whether one is more deeply
affected by a Symphony of Mozart, a tragedy by
Shakespeare, a poem by Uhland, or a Rondo by
Hummel must depend, after all, on the individual
himself.⟯ Those again who hold that music affects
our feelings " directly," whereas the other arts do so
only through the medium of ideas, express the same
error in other words.   For we have already seen
that the excitation of feelings by the beautiful in
music is but one of its indirect effects, our
imagination only being *directly* affected.   Musical
dissertations constantly recall the analogy which
undoubtedly exists between music and *architecture*,
but what architect in his senses ever conceived the
*aim* of architecture to be the excitation of feelings,
or the feelings the *subject-matter* of his art ?

*Every* real work of art appeals to our emotional faculty in some way, but *none* in any exclusive way. No canon peculiar to musical æsthetics only can be deduced from the fact that there is a certain connection between music and the emotions. We might as well study the properties of wine by getting drunk. The crux of the question is the *specific* mode in which *music* affects our feelings. Hence, instead of enlarging on the vague and secondary effects of musical phenomena, we ought to endeavour to penetrate deeply into the spirit of the works themselves, and to explain their effects by the laws of their inherent nature. A poet or painter would hardly persuade himself that when he has ascertained the " feelings " his landscape or drama awakens, he has obtained a rationale of the beauties contained in it. He will seek to discover the source of the irresistible power which makes us enjoy the work in this particular form and in no other. Writers on this subject are by no means justified in confusing emotional impressions and musical beauty (instead of adopting the scientific method of keeping these two factors apart as much as possible) simply because an enquiry of this kind offers in respect of music, as we shall presently see, far greater difficulties than any other art, and because such an enquiry cannot go below a certain depth.

Independently of the fact that our feelings can never become the basis of æsthetic laws, there are many cogent reasons why we should not trust to the feelings aroused by music. As a consequence of our mental constitution, words, titles, and other con-

ventional associations (in sacred, military, and
operatic music more especially) give to our feelings
and thoughts a direction which we often falsely
ascribe to the character of the music itself.  For, in
reality, there is no *causal nexus* between a musical
composition and the feelings it may excite, as the
latter vary with our experience and impressibility.
The present generation often wonder how their fore-
fathers could imagine that just *this* arrangement of
sounds adequately represented just *this* feeling.
We need but instance the effects which works by
Mozart, Beethoven, and Weber produced when they
were new, as compared with their effects on us. How
many compositions by Mozart were thought by his
contemporaries to be the most perfect expression of
passion, warmth, and vigour of which music is
capable.  The placidity and moral sunshine of
Haydn's symphonies were placed in contrast with
the violent bursts of passion, the internal strife, the
bitter and acute grief embodied in Mozart's music.*
Twenty or thirty years later, precisely the same
comparison was made between Beethoven and
Mozart.  Mozart, the emblem of supreme and
transcendent passion, was replaced by Beethoven,
while he himself was promoted to the Olympic
classicalness of Haydn.  Every observant musician

---

* Of Rochlitz, in particular, there are sayings on record about
Mozart's instrumental music, which sound rather strange to our ears.
This same Rochlitz describes the graceful Minuet-Capriccio in
Weber's Sonata in A flat, as "the copious, incessant effusion of a
"passionate and fiercely agitated mind, controlled, withal, by a
"marvellous steadiness of purpose."

will, in the course of his own life, experience analogous changes of taste. The *musical* merit of the many compositions which at one time made so deep an impression, and the æsthetic enjoyment which their originality and *beauty* still yield, are not altered in the least by this dissimilar effect on the feelings at different periods. Thus, there is no invariable and inevitable *nexus* between musical works and certain states of mind; the connection being, on the contrary, of a far more transient kind than in any other art.

It is manifest, therefore, that the effect of music on the emotions does not possess the attributes of inevitableness, exclusiveness, and uniformity that a phenomenon from which æsthetic principles are to be deduced ought to have.

Far be it from us to underrate the deep emotions which music awakens from their slumber, or the feelings of joy or sadness which our minds dreamily experience. It is one of the most precious and inestimable secrets of nature, that an art should have the power of evoking feelings entirely free from worldly associations, and kindled, as it were, by the spark divine. It is only the unscientific proceeding of deducing *æsthetic principles* from such facts against which we protest. Music may, undoubtedly, awaken feelings of great joy or intense sorrow; but might not the same or a still greater effect be produced by the news that we have won the first prize in the lottery, or by the dangerous illness of a friend? So long as we refuse to include lottery tickets among the symphonies, or medical bulletins among the overtures, we must refrain from treating the emotions as an æsthetic monopoly of music in general or a certain piece of music in particular. Everything depends upon the *specific* "modus operandi" *by means of which* music evokes such feelings. The fourth and fifth chapters will be devoted to a critical examination of the influence which music exerts on our feelings, and we shall then have occasion to consider the *positive* aspect of this remarkable connection. In this, the introductory chapter of our work, our object was to throw as much light as possible on its negative aspect as a standing protest against an unscientific principle.

Herbarth (in the ninth chapter of his Encyclopædia) has, to the best of my knowledge, struck the first blow at the theory that the feelings are the foundation of musical æsthetics. After expressing his disapproval of the vague manner in which works of art are criticised, he goes on to say: "Interpreters "of dreams and astrologers have for thousands of "years persistently ignored the fact that people "dream because they are asleep, and that the stars "appear now in one part of the heavens and now in "another, because they are in motion. Similarly, "there are even good musicians who still cling to the "belief that music is capable of expressing definite "feelings, as though the feelings which it accidentally "arouses and to express which music may for this "very reason be employed, were the proximate cause "of the rules of simple and double counterpoint. "For these alone form the groundwork of music. What "subject, we might ask, did the old masters mean to

" illustrate, when they developed all the possible forms
" of the fugue ?   No subject at all.   Their thoughts
" did not travel beyond the• limits of the art, but
" penetrate deeply into its inmost recesses.   He who
" adheres to meanings, thereby betrays his dislike of
" the inner aspect of things and his love of mere
" outward appearance."   It is much to be regretted
that Herbarth refrained from prosecuting these
occasional strictures more in detail, and that along
with these brilliant flashes there  go some rather
questionable  statements;  at  all  events,  we  shall
presently see that the views  we have just quoted
failed to gain the regard they so well merited.

NOTE.—Our  present  purpose,  we  think,  hardly
makes it incumbent on us to mention the authors of
the doctrines  which  it  is  our  object  to  disprove,
these doctrines being not so much the fruit of original
speculation,  as  the  enunciation  of  traditional
convictions that have gained great popularity.   To
show how deeply these doctrines have taken root, we
will  select  some  examples  from  their  vast  number.
The following emanate from the pens both of  old
and modern writers on music :—

MATTHESON.—" When  composing  a  melody,  our
    chief aim should be to illustrate a certain *emotion*
    (if not more than one)."  (*Vollkomm. Capellmeister,*
    page 143.)
NEIDHARDT.—" The  ultimate  aim  of  music  is  to
    rouse *all the passions* by means of sound and rhythm,
    rivalling  the  most  eloquent  oration."   (Preface to
    *Temperatur.*)

J. N. FORKEL understands "figures in music," in the same sense as in poetry or rhetoric—namely, " as the expression of the various modes in "which *sensations* and *emotions* gain utterance." (*Ueber die Theorie der Musik*," Göttingen, 1777, page 26.)

J. MOSEL defines music as "the art of expressing certain emotions through the medium of systematically combined sounds."

C. F. MICHAELIS.—"Music is the art of expressing *sensations* by modulated sounds. It is the language of emotion," &c. (*Ueber den Geist der Tonkunst*, 2nd essay, 1800, page 29.)

MARPURG.—"The composer's task is to copy nature . . . to stir the passions at will . . . to express the living movements of the soul and the cravings of the heart." (*Krit. Musikus*, Vol. I., 1750, § 40.)

W. HEINSE.—"To picture, or rather to rouse the *passions* is the chief and final aim of music." (*Musikal. Dialoge*, 1805, page 30.)

J. J. ENGEL.—"A symphony, a sonata, &c., must be the representation of some passion developed in a variety of forms." (*Ueber musik. Malerei*, 1780, page 29.)

J. PH. KIRNBERGER.—"A melodious phrase (theme) is a phrase taken from the language of emotion. It induces in a sensitive listener the same state of mind which gave birth to it." (*Kunst des reinen Satzes*, Part II., page 152.)

PIERER'S *Universallexicon* (2nd edition).—" Music
is the art of expressing sensations and states of
mind by means of pleasing sounds.   It is superior
to *poetry* because the latter can only (!) describe
emotions which the intellect apprehends, whereas
music expresses vague and undefinable emotions
and sensations."

G. SCHILLING'S *Universallexicon der Tonkunst*
gives a similar explanation under the heading
" Musik."

KOCH defines music as " the art of suggesting trains
of pleasurable feelings through the medium of
sound."

A. ANDRÉ.—" Music is the art of producing sounds
capable of expressing, exciting, and sustaining
feelings and passions."   (*Lehrbuch der Tonkunst*, I.)

SULZER.—" While language expresses our feelings
in words, music expresses them by sounds."
(*Theorie der Schönen Künste.*)

J. W. BŒHM.—" Not to the intellect do the sweet
strains of music appeal, but to our *emotional faculty*
only."   (*Analyse des Schönen der Musik*, Vienna,
1830, page 62.)

GOTTFRIED WEBER.—" Music is the art of expressing *emotions* through the medium of sound."
(*Theorie der Tonsetzkunst*, 2nd edition, Vol. I.,
page 15.)

F. HAND.—" Music represents *emotions*.  *Each feeling and each state of mind* has its own inherent
sound and rhythm, and these have their objective
counterpart in music."   (*Æsthetik der Tonkunst*,
Vol. I., 1837, § 24.)

AMADEUS AUTODIDAKTUS.—"Music has its origin and its roots in the world of *sentiment* and *sensation*. Musically melodious sounds (!) are a sealed book to the intellect, which only describes and analyzes sensations. . . . They appeal to the *feelings*," &c. (*Aphorismen über Musik*, Leipzig, 1847, page 329.)

FERMO BELLINI.—" Music is the art of expressing sentiments and passions through the medium of sound." (*Manuale di Musica*, Milano, Ricordi, 1853.)

FRIEDRICH THIERSCH.—*Allgemeine Æsthetik*, Berlin, 1846, § 18, page 101 : " Music is the art of expressing, and of exciting feelings and emotions by groups of selected sounds."

A. v. DOMMER.—*Elemente der Musik*, Leipzig, 1862. *" The object of Music :* Music is to awaken our *feelings*, and these, in their turn, are to raise up *images* in the mind." (Page 174.)

RICHARD WAGNER.—*Das Kunstwerk der Zukunft* (1850, Select Works, III., 99—similar passages occurring in his other writings).—" The organ of the *emotions* is *sound*, its intentionally æsthetic language is music." In Wagner's later writings his definitions become still more obscure ; music being there for him " the art of expression in the abstract " (" Oper und Drama," Coll. Writings III., 343), which, as a " conception of the Universe," he deems capable of " comprehending the essence of things in its immediate manifestation," &c. (" Beethoven," 1870, page 6, &c.)

# CHAPTER II.

THE proposition that the *feelings* are the *subject* which music has to represent is due partly to the theory according to which the *ultimate aim* of music is to excite feelings, and partly to an amended form of this theory.

A philosophical disquisition into an art demands a clear definition of its *subject-matter*. The diversity of the subject-matter of the various arts and the fundamental difference in the mode of treatment, are a natural sequence of the dissimilarity of the *senses* to which they severally appeal. Every art comprises a range of ideas, which it expresses after its own fashion, in sound, language, colour, stone, &c. A work of art, therefore, endows a definite conception with a material form of beauty. This definite conception, its embodiment, and the union of both, are the conditions of an æsthetic ideal, with which a critical examination into every art is indissolubly connected.

The subject of a poem, a painting, or statue may be expressed in words and reduced to ideas. We say, for instance, this picture represents a flower-girl, this statue a gladiator, this poem one of Roland's exploits. Upon the more or less perfect embodiment of the particular subject in the artist's production depends our verdict respecting the beauty of the work of art.

The whole gamut of human *feelings* has with almost complete unanimity been proclaimed to be *the subject of music*, since the emotions were thought to be in antithesis to the definiteness of intellectual conceptions. This was supposed to be the feature by which the musical ideal is distinguished from the ideal of the other fine arts and poetry. According to this theory, therefore, sound and its ingenious combinations are but the material and the medium of expression, by which the composer represents love, courage, piety, and delight. The innumerable varieties of emotion constitute the idea which, on being translated into sound, assumes the form of a musical composition. The beautiful melody and the skilful harmony as such, do not charm us, but only what they imply: the whispering of love, or the clamour of ardent combatants.

In order to escape from such vague notions, we must, first of all, sever from their habitual associations metaphors of the above description. The *whispering* may be expressed, true; but not the whispering of "love"; the *clamour* may be reproduced, undoubtedly; but not the clamour of "ardent combatants." Music may reproduce phenomena such as whispering, storming, roaring, but the feelings of love or anger have only a subjective existence.

Definite feelings and emotions are unsusceptible of being embodied in music.

Our emotions have no isolated existence in the mind, and cannot, therefore, be evoked by an art which is incapable of representing the remaining series of mental states. They are, on the contrary,

c

dependent on physiological and pathological conditions, on notions and judgments; in fact, on all
the processes of human reasoning which so many
conceive as antithetical to the emotions.

What then transforms an indefinite feeling into a
*definite* one—into the feeling of longing, hope, or
love ?  Is it the mere degree of intensity; the
fluctuating rate of inner motion ? Assuredly not.
The latter may be the same in the case of dissimilar
feelings, or may, in the case of the same feeling,
vary with the time and the person.  Only by virtue
of ideas and judgments—unconscious though we
may be of. them when our feelings run high—can an
indefinite state of mind pass into a definite feeling.
The feeling of hope is inseparable from the conception of a happier state that is to come, and which
we compare with the actual state.  The feeling of
sadness involves the notion of a past state of
happiness.  These are perfectly definite ideas or
conceptions, and in default of them—*the apparatus of
thought,* as it were—no feeling can be called "hope"
or "sadness," for through them alone can a feeling
assume a definite character.  On excluding these
conceptions from consciousness, nothing remains but
a vague sense of motion which at best could not
rise above a general feeling of satisfaction or discomfort.  The feeling of *love* cannot be conceived
apart from the image of the beloved being, or apart
from the desire and the longing for the possession of
the object of our affections.  It is not the kind of
psychical activity, but the intellectual substratum,
the subject underlying it, which constitutes it *love.*

Dynamically speaking, love may be gentle or impetuous, buoyant or depressed, and yet it remains
love. This reflection alone ought to make it clear
that music can express only those qualifying
adjectives, and not the substantive, love, itself. A
determinate feeling (a passion, an emotion) as such,
never exists without a definable meaning, which
can, of course, only be communicated through the
medium of definite ideas. Now, since music as an
"indefinite form of speech" is admittedly incapable
of expressing definite ideas, is it not a psychologically
unavoidable conclusion, that it is likewise incapable
of expressing definite emotions? For the *definite
character* of an emotion rests entirely on the
meaning involved in it.

How it is that music *may*, nevertheless, awaken
feelings (though not necessarily so) such as sadness,
joy, &c., we shall try to explain hereafter, when we
come to examine music from a subjective point of
view. At this stage of our enquiry it is enough to
determine whether music is capable of *representing*
any definite emotion whatever. To this question
only a negative answer can be given, the definiteness
of an emotion being inseparably connected with
concrete notions and conceptions, and to reduce
these to a material form is altogether beyond the
power of music. A certain class of *ideas*, however,
is quite susceptible of being adequately expressed by
means which unquestionably belong to the sphere of
music proper. This class comprises all ideas which,
consistently with the organ to which they appeal,
are associated with audible changes of strength,

motion, and ratio: the ideas of intensity waxing and
diminishing; of motion hastening and lingering; of
ingeniously complex and simple progression, &c.
The æsthetic expression of music may be described
by terms such as graceful, gentle, violent, vigorous,
elegant, fresh; all these ideas being expressible by
corresponding modifications of sound. We may,
therefore, use those adjectives as directly describing
*musical* phenomena, without thinking of the ethical
meanings attaching to them in a psychological sense,
and which, from the habit of associating ideas, we
readily ascribe to the effect of the music, or mistake
even for purely musical properties.

The ideas which a composer expresses are mainly
and primarily of a *purely musical* nature. His
imagination conceives a definite and graceful melody
aiming at nothing beyond itself. Every concrete
phenomenon suggests the class to which it belongs,
or some still wider conception in which the latter is
included, and by continuing this process, the idea of
the absolute is reached at last. This is true also of
musical phenomena. This melodious Adagio, for
instance, softly dying away, suggests the ideas of
gentleness and concord *in the abstract*. Our
imaginative faculty, ever ready to establish relations
between the conceptions of art and our sentiments,
may construe these softly-ebbing strains of music
in a still loftier sense—*e.g.*, as the placid resignation
of a mind at peace with itself, and they *may* rouse
even a vague sense of everlasting rest.

The primary aim of Poetry, Sculpture, and
Painting is likewise to produce some concrete image.

Only by way of inference can the picture of a flower-girl call up the wider notion of maidenly content and modesty; the picture of a snow-covered churchyard the transitoriness of earthly existence. In like manner, but far more vaguely and capriciously, may the listener discover in a piece of music the idea of youthful contentedness or that of transitoriness. These abstract *notions*, however, are by no means the subject-matter of the pictures or the musical compositions, and it is still more absurd to talk as if the *feelings* of "transitoriness" or of "youthful contentedness" could be represented by them.

There are *ideas* which, though not occurring as *feelings*, are yet capable of being fully expressed by music; and conversely, there are *feelings* which affect our minds, but which are so constituted as to defy their adequate expression by any *ideas* which music can represent.

*What* part of the feelings, then, can music represent, if not the subject involved in them?

Only their *dynamic* properties. It may reproduce the motion accompanying psychical action, according to its momentum: speed, slowness, strength, weakness, increasing and decreasing intensity. But motion is only one of the concomitants of feeling, not the feeling itself. It is a popular fallacy to suppose that the descriptive power of music is sufficiently qualified by saying that, although incapable of representing the *subject* of a feeling, it may represent the feeling itself—not the object of love, but the "feeling of love." In reality, however, music can do neither. It cannot reproduce the feeling of love, but only the element of motion, and this may occur in any other feeling just as well as in love, and in no case is it the distinctive feature. The term "love" is as abstract as "virtue" or "immortality," and it is quite superfluous to assure us that music is unable to express abstract notions. *No* art can do this, for it is a matter of course that only definite and concrete ideas (those that have assumed a living form, as it were) can be incorporated by an art.* But no instrumental composition can describe the ideas of love, wrath, or fear, since there is no *causal nexus* between these ideas and certain combinations of sound. Which of the elements inherent in these ideas, then, does music turn to account so effectually? Only the element of *motion*—in the wider sense, of course, according to which the increasing and decreasing force of a single note or chord is "motion" also. This is the element which music has in common with our emotions, and which, with creative power, it contrives to exhibit in an endless variety of forms and contrasts.

Though the idea of *motion* appears to us a most far-reaching and important one, it has hitherto been conspicuously disregarded in all enquiries into the nature and action of music.

Whatever else there is in music that apparently pictures states of feeling, is *symbolical.*

---

* Vischer (*Aesth.*, § 11, Note) defines determinate ideas as the domains of life, provided that the corresponding realities be assumed to agree with our conceptions. For conception always denotes the pure and faultless image of the reality.

Sounds, like colours, are originally associated in our minds with certain symbolical meanings, which produce their effects independently of, and antecedently to any design of art. Every colour has a character of its own ; it is not a mere cipher into which the artist blows the breath of life, but a force. Between it and certain states of mind Nature herself has established a sympathetic connection. Are we not all acquainted with the unsophisticated meanings of colours, so dear to the popular imagination, and which cultured minds have exalted into poetic refinement ? Green is associated with a feeling of hope, blue with fidelity. Rosenkranz recognises "graceful dignity" in orange, "philistine politeness" in violet, &c. ("Psychologie," 2nd edition, page 102.)

In like manner, the first elements of music, such as the various keys, chords, and "timbres," have severally a character of their own. There exists, in fact, a but too ready art of interpreting the meanings of musical elements. Schubart's symbolism of the keys in music forms a counterpart, as it were, to Goethe's interpretation of colours. Such elements (sounds, colours), however, when employed for the purposes of art, are subject to laws quite distinct from those upon which the effect of their isolated action depends. When looking at a historical painting we should never think of construing the red appearing in it as always meaning joy, or the white as always meaning innocence. Just as little in a symphony would the key of A flat major always awaken romantic feelings, or the key of B minor always misanthropic ones, every triad a feeling of satisfaction, and every diminished seventh a feeling of despair. Æsthetically speaking, such primordially distinctive traits are non-existent when viewed by the light of those wider laws to which they are subordinate. The relation in question cannot, for a moment, be assumed to *express* or *represent* anything definite whatsoever. We called it "symbolical" because the subject is exhibited not directly, but in a form essentially different from it. If yellow is the emblem of jealousy, the key of G major that of gaiety, the cypress that of mourning, such interpretations, and the definite character of our emotions, imply a psycho-physiological relation. The colour, the sound, or the plant as such, are not related to our emotions, but only the meanings we ourselves attach to them. We cannot, therefore, speak of an isolated chord as representing a determinate feeling, and much less can we do so when it occurs in a connected piece of music.

Beyond the analogy of motion, and the symbolism of sounds, music possesses no means for fulfilling its alleged mission.

Seeing then how easy it is to deduce from the inherent nature of sound the inability of music to represent definite emotions, it seems almost incredible that our every-day experience should, nevertheless, have failed to firmly establish this fact. Let those who, when listening to some instrumental composition, imagine the strings to quiver with a profusion of feeling, clearly show *what* feeling is the subject of the music. The experiment is indispensable. If, for instance, we

were to listen to Beethoven's Overture to " Prometheus," an attentive and musical ear would
successively discover more or' less the following:
the notes of the first bar, after a fall into the lower
fourth, rise gently and in rapid succession; a move-
ment repeated in the second bar. The third and
fourth bars continue it in wider limits. The jet
propelled by the fountain comes trickling down in
drops, but rises once more, only to repeat in the
following four bars the figure of the preceding four.
The listener thus perceives that the first and second
bars of the *melody* are symmetrical ; that these two
bars and the succeeding two are likewise so, and that
the same is true of the wider arc of the first four
bars and the corresponding arc of the following four.
The bass which indicates the *rhythm* marks the
beginning of each of the first three bars with one
single beat, the fourth with two beats, while the
same rotation is observed in the next four bars.
The fourth bar, therefore, is different from the first
three, and this point of difference becoming symmetrical, through being repeated in the following
four bars, agreeably impresses the ear, as an un-
expected development within .the former limits.
The *harmony* of the theme exhibits the same correspondence of one large and two small arcs : the
common chord of C of the first four bars corresponds
to the chord of $\frac{6}{4}$ of the fifth and sixth, and to the
chord of $\frac{6}{5}$ of the seventh and eighth bars.   This
systematic correspondence of melody, rhythm, and
harmony results in a structure composed of parts at
once symmetrical and dissimilar, into which further

gradations of light and shade are introduced through the "timbre" peculiar to each instrument and the varying volume of sound :—

Any other *subject* than the one alluded to we absolutely fail to find in the theme, and still less could we mention a *feeling* it represents, or necessarily arouses in the listener.   An analysis of this kind reduces, it is true, to a skeleton, a body glowing with life ; it destroys the beauty, but at the same time it destroys all false constructions.

No other theme of instrumental music will fare any better than the one which we have selected at random.

A numerous class of lovers of music think that it
is a characteristic feature of the older "classical"
music only, to disregard the representation of feelings,
and it is at once admitted that no feeling can be
shown to form the subject of the forty-eight Preludes
and Fugues of J. S. Bach's "well-tempered clavi-
chord." However glaringly unscientific and arbitrary
such a distinction may be—a distinction, by the way,
which has its explanation in the fact that the older
music affords still more unmistakable proof that it
aims at nothing beyond itself, and that interpretations of the kind mentioned would, in this case,
present more obstacles than attractions—this alone
is enough to prove that music need not *necessarily*
awaken feelings, or that it must *necessarily* be the
object of music to represent them.    The whole
domain of florid counterpoint would then have to be
ignored.    But if large departments of art, which can
be defended both on historical and æsthetic grounds,
have to be passed over for the sake of a theory,* it
may be concluded that such a theory is false.
Though a single leak will sink a ship, those who are
not content with that, are at liberty to knock out the
whole bottom.    Let them play the theme of a
Symphony by Mozart or Haydn, an Adagio by
Beethoven, a Scherzo by Mendelssohn, one of
Schumann's or Chopin's compositions for the

---

* Disciples of Bach, such as Spitta, attempt to remove the difficulty,
not indeed by questioning the theory itself, but by ascribing to his
fugues and chords an emotional element, as eloquent and positive as
the most ardent admirer of Beethoven ever detected in the latter's
Sonatas.  This is consistent, at all events!

piano, anything, in short, from the stock of our
standard music ; or again, the most popular themes
from Overtures of Auber, Donizetti, and Flotow. Who
would be bold enough to point out a definite feeling
as the subject of any of these themes ?   One will say
" love."  He may be right.   Another thinks it is
" longing."   Perhaps so.   A third feels it to be
" religious fervour."   Who can contradict him ?
Now, how can we talk of a definite feeling being
*represented*, when nobody really knows *what* is
represented ?   Probably all will agree about the
beauty or beauties of the composition, whereas all
will differ regarding its subject.  To *represent* something is to clearly exhibit it ; to distinctly set it
before us.  But how can we call *that* the subject
*represented* by an art, which is really its vaguest and
most indefinite element, and which must, therefore,
for ever remain highly debatable ground ?

We have intentionally selected examples from
*instrumental music*, for only what is true of the latter
is true also of music as such.   If we wish to decide
the question whether music possesses the character
of definiteness, what its nature and properties are,
and what its limits and tendencies, no other than
instrumental music can be taken into consideration.
What *instrumental music* is unable to achieve, lies
also beyond the pale of *music proper ;* for it alone is
pure and self-subsistent music.   No matter whether
we regard vocal music as superior to, or more
effective than instrumental music—an unscientific
proceeding, by the way, which is generally the
upshot of one-sided dilettantism—we cannot help

admitting that the term "music," in its true meaning, must exclude compositions in which words are set to music. In vocal or operatic music it is impossible to draw so nice a distinction between the effect of the music, and that of the words, that an exact definition of the share which each has had in the production of the whole becomes practicable. An enquiry into the subject of music must leave out even compositions with inscriptions, or so-called programme-music. Its union with poetry, though enhancing the power of music, does not widen its limits.*

---

* Gervinus in his work " Händel und Shakespeare " (1868) has re-opened the controversy respecting the superiority of vocal over instrumental music; but when he calls "vocal music," "true and genuine music," and " instrumental music " a product of art which has "lost the spirit of life and has degenerated into a mere out-ward display," a physical agent for the production of physiological stimuli, he affords the proof, all his ingenuity notwithstanding, that a learned Handel-enthusiast may, at the same time, fall into the most singular errors in regard to the true nature of music. Nobody has ever exposed these fallacies more plainly than Ferdinand Hiller, from whose critique on Gervinus' work we select the following notable passages:—" The union of word and sound may be of many " different kinds. What a variety of combinations lie between the " most simple and almost spoken recitative and a chorus of Bach or " a *Finale* in one of Mozart's operas ! But words and music affect " the listener with *equal* force only in the recitative, whether occur-" ring by itself, or as a mere exclamation in the midst of a song. " Whenever music steps forth in its true character, it leaves language, " potent language, far behind. The reason (*unfortunately*, one feels " almost tempted to say) is not far to seek. Even the most wretched " poem, when set to beautiful music, can scarcely lessen the enjoy-" ment to be derived from the latter, whereas the most exquisite " poetry fails to compensate for dulness in the musical part. How " slender is the interest which the words of an Oratorio excite—it is " difficult to comprehend how the gifted composer could ever extract

Vocal music is an undecomposable compound, and it is impossible to gauge the relative importance of each of its constituents. In discussing the effect of *poetry*, nobody, surely, will quote the *opera* as an example. Now, it requires a greater effort, but no deeper insight, to follow the same line of thought when the fundamental principles of musical æsthetics are in question.

Vocal music colours, as it were, the poetic drawing.* In the musical elements we were able to

---

" from them the material for music that fascinates our hearts and " minds for hours together. Nay, we go still farther, and maintain " that the listener as a rule is quite unable to grasp both the words " and the music at the same time. The conventional sounds which " go to build up a sentence in speech must be united in rapid " succession, so that our memory may hold them together, while ' they reach the intellect. Music, on the other hand, impresses the " listener with the first note and carries him away without giving him " the time, nay, the possibility, of reverting to what he has just " heard. . . . Whether we listen to the most simple Volks- " lied," Hiller continues, " or are overpowered by Handel's Hallelujah " Chorus, sung by a thousand voices, our delight and enthusiasm are " due, in the former case, to the melodious bud that has hardly yet " expanded into a flower; in the latter, to the power and grandeur of " the combined elements of a whole universe of sound. The fact " that one treats of a sweetheart, the other of a world of bliss, in no " way helps to produce the primary and instantaneous effect. For " this effect is a purely musical one and would be produced even " though we did not, or could not understand the words." (*Aus dem Tonleben unserer Zeit, Neue Folge* (Leipzig, 1871), page 40, &c.

* This well-known figure of speech is relevant only so long as nothing but the abstract relations between music and words are referred to, quite irrespective of *æsthetic* requirements, and when the only point to be settled is on which of these two factors the exact and definite meaning of the *subject* depends. It ceases, however, to be appropriate when the point at issue is, not this abstract relation,

discover the most brilliant and delicate hues, and an abundance of symbolic meanings. Though by their aid it might be possible to transform a second-rate poem into a passionate effusion of the soul, it is not the music, but the words which *determine* the subject of a vocal composition. Not the colouring, but the drawing renders the represented subject intelligible. We appeal to the listener's faculty of abstraction, and beg him to think, in a purely musical sense, of some dramatically effective melody, *apart* from the context. A melody, for instance, which impresses us as highly dramatic, and which is intended to represent the feeling of *rage*, can express this state of mind in no other way than by quick and impetuous

---

but the mode in which the musical material is manipulated. Only in a *logical* (one might almost say " judicial ") sense can the words be said to be the essence, and music a mere accessory. The *æsthetic* demands on the composer are of a far loftier kind and can only be satisfied by purely *musical beauty* (suited, of course, to the words). When, therefore, we have not to establish in the abstract what music does on being joined to words, but how it *ought to set about* in actual experience, we must above all beware of making it the handmaid of poetry and thus make it move within the narrow limits which the drawer sets to the colourist. Ever since Gluck, during the great and salutary reaction against the melodious exaggerations of the Italian School, retreated even *beyond* the golden mean (just as Richard Wagner has done in our own days), the saying that the words are the " correct and well sketched drawing " which music has but to colour (a remark which occurs in the dedication to "Alceste ") has been repeated *ad nauseam*. If music is to poetry no more than the mere colourist—if in its dual capacity of drawer and colourist it fails to contribute something entirely new, which by the inherent power of its beauty sends forth living shoots of its own and reduces the words to a mere framework, then it has reached at best the level of a student's exercise or an amateur's standard of excellence, but not the sublime height of true art.

motion. Words expressing passionate *love*, though diametrically opposed in meaning, might, therefore, be suitably rendered by the same melody.

At a time when thousands (among whom there were men like Jean Jacques Rousseau) were moved to tears by the air from " Orpheus "—

> " J'ai perdu mon Eurydice,
> Rien n'égale mon malheur,"

Boyé, a contemporary of Gluck, observed that precisely the same melody would accord equally well, if not better, with words conveying exactly the reverse, thus—

> " J'ai trouvé mon Eurydice,
> Rien n'égale mon bonheur."

The following is the beginning of the Aria in question, which, for the sake of brevity, we give with piano accompaniment, but in all other respects exactly as the original Italian score :—

ORFEO.
*Vivace.*

Che fa - rò sen-za Eu-ri - di-ce! do-ve an-drò sen-za il mio

ben! che fa - rò, do-ve an - drò; che fa -

- rò   sen - za il   mio   ben,   do - ve an-

- drò   sen - za il   mio   ben.

We, for our part, are not of opinion that in this case the composer is quite free from blame, inasmuch as music most assuredly possesses accents which more truly express a feeling of profound sorrow. If, however, from among innumerable instances, we selected the one quoted, we have done so, because, in the first place, it affects the composer who is credited with the greatest dramatic accuracy; and, secondly, because several generations hailed *this very melody* as most correctly rendering the supreme grief which the *words* express.

But even far more definite and expressive passages from vocal music, when considered apart from the text, enable us at best to *guess* the feeling they are intended to convey. They resemble a silhouette, the original of which we recognise only after being told whose likeness it is.

What is true of isolated passages is true also in a wider application. There are many cases where an

D

entirely new text has been employed for a complete
musical work.  If Meyerbeer's "Huguenots," after
changing the scene of action, the time, the
characters, and the plot, were to be performed as
"The Ghibellines of Pisa," though so clumsy an
adaptation would, undoubtedly, produce a disagreeable impression, the purely musical part would
in no way suffer.  And yet the religious feeling and
fanaticism which are entirely wanting in "The
Ghibellines" are supposed to be the motive power in
"The Huguenots."  Luther's hymn must not be
cited as counter-evidence, as it is merely a *quotation.*
From a musical point of view it consists with any
profession of faith whatever.  Has the reader ever
heard the *Allegro fugato* from the Overture to
"The Magic Flute" changed into a vocal quartet
of quarrelling Jewish pedlars?  Mozart's music,
though not altered in the smallest degree, fits the low
text appallingly well, and the enjoyment we derive
from the gravity of the music in the opera can be no
heartier than our laugh at the farcical humour of the
parody.  We might quote numberless instances of
the plastic character of every musical theme and
every human emotion.  The feeling of religious
fervour is rightly considered to be the least liable to
musical misconstruction.  Yet there are countless
village and country churches in Germany in which
at Eucharist pieces like Proch's "Alpine Horn,"
or the *Finale* from the "Sonnambula" (with
the coquettish leap to the tenth) are performed
on the organ.  Foreigners who visit churches in Italy
hear, to their amazement, the most popular themes

from operas by Rossini, Bellini, Donizetti, and Verdi.
Pieces like these and of a still more secular character, provided they do not lose the quality of
sobriety altogether, are far from interfering with
the devotions of the congregation, who, on the
contrary, appear to be greatly edified.  If music, as
such, were capable of representing the feeling of
piety, a *quid pro quo* of this kind would be as un-
likely as the contingency of a preacher reciting from
the pulpit a novel by Tieck or an Act of Parliament.
The greatest masters of sacred music afford abundant examples in proof of our proposition.  Handel,
in particular, set to work with the greatest noncha-
lance in this respect.  Winterfeld has shown that
many of the most celebrated airs from " The
Messiah," including those most of all admired as
being especially suggestive of piety, have been
taken from secular duets (mostly erotic) composed
in the years 1711-1712, when Handel set to music
certain *Madrigals by Mauro Ortensio* for the Electoral
Princess Caroline of Hanover.  The music of the
second duet :

> " No, di voi non vo' fidarmi,
> Cieco amor, crudel beltà;
> Troppo siete menzognere
> Lusinghiere deità ! "

Handel employed unaltered both in key and melody
for the chorus in the first part of " The Messiah,"
" For unto us a Child is born."  The third part of
the same duet, " Sò per prova i vostri inganni,"
contains the same themes which occur in the chorus
of the second part of " The Messiah," " All we like

sheep." The music of the Madrigal, No. 16 (duet for soprano and alto), is essentially the same as the duet from the third part of " The Messiah," " Oh death, where is thy sting ? " But the words of the madrigal are as follows :

> " Se tu non lasci amore
> Mio cor, ti pentirai
> Lo sò ben io ! "

There is a vast number of similar instances, but we need here only refer to the entire series of pastoral pieces from the " Christmas " Oratorio, which, as is well known, were naïvely taken from *secular* cantatas composed for special occasions. And Gluck, whose music, we are taught, attained the sublime height of dramatic accuracy, only by every note being scrupulously adapted to each special case, nay, by the melodies being extracted from the very rhythm of the syllables—Gluck has transferred to his " Armida " no fewer than five airs from his earlier Italian operas (compare with the author's " Moderne Oper," page 16). It is obvious, therefore, that *vocal music*, which in theory can never determine the principles of music proper, is likewise, in practice, powerless to call in question the canons which experience has established for instrumental music.

The proposition which we are endeavouring to disprove has become, as it were, part and parcel of current musical æsthetics, so that all derivative and collateral theories enjoy the same reputation of invulnerability. To the latter belongs the theory that music is able to reproduce visual and auditory impressions of a non-musical nature. Whenever the question of the representation of objects by musical means (Tonmalerei) is under debate, we are, with an air of wisdom, assured over and over again that though music is unable to portray *phenomena* which are foreign to its province, it, nevertheless, may picture the *feeling* which they excite. The very reverse is the case. Music can undertake to imitate objective phenomena only, and never the specific feeling they arouse. The falling of snow, the fluttering of birds, and the rising of the sun can be painted musically only, by producing auditory impressions which are dynamically related to those phenomena. In point of strength, pitch, velocity, and rhythm, sounds present to the ear a *figure*, bearing that degree of analogy to certain visual impressions which sensations of various kinds bear to one another. As there is, physiologically speaking, such a thing as a vicarious function (up to a certain point), so may sense-impressions, æsthetically speaking, become vicarious also. There is a well-founded analogy between motion in space and motion in time, between the colour, texture, and size of an object and the pitch, "timbre," and strength of a tone, and it is for this reason quite practicable to paint an object musically. The pretension, however, to describe by musical means the "feeling" which the falling snow, the crowing cock, or a flash of lightning excites in us, is simply ludicrous.

Although, as far as we remember, all musical theorists tacitly accept, and base their arguments on the postulate, that music has the power of

representing definite emotions—yet, their better judgment has kept them from openly avowing it.  The
conspicuous absence of *definite ideas* in music troubled
their minds and induced them to lay down the somewhat modified principle that the object of music
was to awaken and represent "indefinite," not
definite emotions.  Rationally understood, this can
only mean that music ought to deal with the *motion*
accompanying a feeling, regardless of its essential
part, with what is felt ; in other words, that its
function is restricted to the reproduction of what
we termed the *dynamic* element of an emotion, a
function which we unhesitatingly conceded to music.
But this property does not enable music "to
represent indefinite feelings," for to "represent"
something "indefinite" is a contradiction in
terms.  Psychical motion, considered as motion
apart from the state of mind it involves, can
never become the object of an art, because without
an answer to the query: what is moving, or what
is being moved, an art has nothing tangible to
work upon.  That which is implied in the
proposition—namely, that music is not intended to
represent a *definite* feeling (which is undoubtedly
true) is only a negative aspect of the question.  But
what is the positive, the creative factor, in a musical
composition ?  An indefinite feeling as such, cannot
supply a *subject;* to utilise it, an art would, first of
all, have to solve the problem : What *form* can be
given to it ?  The function of art consists in *in-
dividualising*, in evolving the definite out of the
indefinite, the particular out of the general.  The

theory respecting "indefinite feelings" would reverse this process. It lands us in even greater difficulties than the theory that music represents something, though it is impossible to define what. This position is but a step removed from the clear recognition that music represents *no feelings*, either definite or indefinite. Yet, where is the musician who would deprive his art of that domain which from time immemorial has been claimed as belonging to it ? *

This conclusion might give rise to the view that the representation of definite feelings by music, though impracticable, may yet be adopted as an ideal, never wholly realisable, but which it is possible, and even necessary, to approach more and more closely. The many high-sounding phrases respecting the tendency of music to cast off its vagueness and to become concrete speech, no less than the fulsome praises bestowed on compositions aiming, or supposed to be aiming at this, are a proof of the popularity of the theory in question.

Having absolutely denied the possibility of representing emotions by musical means, we must be

---

* What absurdities arise from the fallacy, which makes us look in every piece of music for the expression of definite feelings or from the still greater misconception of establishing a *causal nexus* between certain forms of music and certain feelings, may be gleaned from the works of so keen-witted a man as Mattheson. Arguing from his doctrine that our principal aim when composing a " melody should be the expression of an emotion," he says in his " *Vollkommener Capellmeister* " (page 230, &c.) : " A Couranto should convey hopefulness." " The Saraband has to express no other feeling than awe." " Voluptuousness reigns supreme in the Concerto grosso." The Chaconne, he contends, should express " satiety " ; the Overture " magnanimity."

still more emphatic in refuting the fallacy which considers it the *æsthetic touchstone* of music.

The *beautiful* in music would not depend on the accurate representation of feelings even if such a representation were *possible.* Let us, for argument's sake, assume the possibility and examine it from a practical point of view.

It is manifestly out of the question to test this fallacy by *instrumental music*, as the latter could be shown to represent definite feelings only by arguing in a circle. We must, therefore, make the experiment with *vocal music*, as being that music whose office it is to emphasize clearly defined states of mind.*

Here the *words* determine the subject to be described; music may give it life and breath, and impart to it a more or less distinct individuality. This is done by utilising as far as possible the characteristics peculiar to motion and the symbols associated with sounds. If greater attention is bestowed on the words than on the production of purely musical beauty, a high degree of individuality may be secured—nay, the delusion may even arise that the music alone expresses the emotion which, though susceptible of intensification, was already immutably contained in the words. Such a tendency is

---

* In his critiques on vocal music, the author (in common with other critics who share his opinion), for the sake of brevity and convenience, has often when speaking of music made use, without any after-thought, of terms such as "express," "describe," "represent," &c. Now such terms may without any impropriety be employed so long as we do not lose sight of their conditional applicability—*i.e.*, of their applicability in a metaphorical and dynamic sense only.

in its consequences on a par with the alleged practicability of *representing* a certain feeling as the subject of a given " piece of music." Suppose there did exist perfect congruity between the real and the assumed power of music; that it was possible to represent feelings by musical means, and that these feelings were the subject of musical compositions. If this assumption be granted, we should be logically compelled to call *such* compositions the best as perform the task in the most *perfect manner*. Yet do we not all know compositions of exquisite beauty *without* any definite subject ? We need but instance Bach's Preludes and Fugues. On the other hand, there are vocal compositions which aim at the most accurate expression of certain emotions, within the limits referred to, and in which the supreme goal is *truthfulness* in this descriptive process. On close examination we find that the rigour with which music is subordinated to words is generally in an inverse ratio to the independent beauty of the former; otherwise expressed, that *rhetorico-dramatical precision* and *musical perfection* go together but half-way, and then proceed in different directions.

The *recitative* affords a good illustration of this truth, since it is that form of music which best accommodates itself to rhetorical requirements, down to the very accent of each individual word ; never even attempting to be more than a faithful copy of rapidly-changing states of mind. This, therefore, in strict accordance with the theory before us, should be the highest and most perfect music. But in the Recitative music degenerates into a mere shadow and relinquishes its individual sphere of action altogether. Is not this a proof that the representing of definite states of mind is contrary to the nature of music, and that in their ultimate bearings they are antagonistic to one another? Let anyone play a long Recitative, leaving out the words, and enquire into its musical merit and subject. *Any kind of music* claiming to be the *sole* factor in producing a given effect should be able to stand this test.

This is true, by no means, of the Recitative alone; the most elevated and excellent forms of music equally bear out the assertion that the *beautiful* tends to disappear in proportion as the *expression of some specific feeling* is aimed at; for the former can expand only if untrammeled by alien factors, whereas the latter relegates music to a subservient place.

We will now ascend from the declamatory principle in the Recitative to the dramatic principle in the Opera. In Mozart's operas there is perfect congruity between the music and the words. Even the most intricate parts, the *Finales*, are beautiful if judged as a whole, quite apart from the words, although certain portions in the middle might without them become somewhat obscure. To do justice in a like degree, both to the musical and the dramatic requirements, is rightly considered to be the ideal of the Opera. But that for this reason there should be perpetual *warfare* between the principles of dramatic nicety and musical beauty, entailing never-ending concessions on both sides, has, to my knowledge, never been conclusively demonstrated. The principle involved in the Opera is not undermined or

weakened by the fact that all the parts are *sung*—
our imagination being easily reconciled to an illusion
of this kind—but it is the constraint imposed alike
upon music and words that leads to continual acts of
trespass or concession, and reduces the opera, as
it were, to a constitutional government, whose very
existence depends upon an incessant struggle between
two parties, equally entitled to power.  It is from
this conflict, in which the composer allows now one
principle and now the other to prevail, whence arise
all the imperfections of the opera, and whence, at the
same time, all rules important for *operatic* works are
deduced.  The principles in which music and the
drama are grounded, if pushed to their logical consequences, are mutually destructive ; but they point
in so similar a direction that they appear almost
*parallel.*

The *dance* is a similar case in point, of which
any ballet is a proof.  The more the graceful
rhythm of the figures is sacrificed in the attempt to
*speak* by gesture and dumb-show, and to convey
definite thoughts and emotions, the closer is the
approximation to the low rank of mere pantomime.
The prominence given to the dramatic principle in
the dance proportionately lessens its rhythmical and
plastic beauty.  The Opera can never be *quite* on a
level with a recited drama, or with purely instrumental music.  A good opera composer will,
therefore, constantly endeavour to combine and
reconcile the two factors, instead of axiomatically
emphasizing now one and now the other.  When in
doubt, however, he will always allow the claim of

*music* to prevail, the chief element in the Opera being not dramatic, but musical beauty. This is evident from the different attitudes of mind in which we listen to a play or an opera in which the same subject is treated. The neglect of the musical part will always be far more keenly felt.*

To us it appears that the importance, as regards the history of the art of music, of the celebrated controversy between the disciples of *Gluck* and those of *Piccini* lies in the fact that the question of the internal conflict in the *Opera*, caused by the incompatibility of the musical and the dramatic principles, was then, for the first time, thoroughly discussed. The controversy, it is true, was carried on without a clear perception of the immense influence which the issue would have on the whole mode of thinking. He who does not shrink from the labour—a very profitable labour, by the way—of tracing this musical

---

* What Mozart says about the *relative positions of music and poetry* in the Opera is highly characteristic of him. Completely opposed to Gluck, who gave poetry precedence of music, Mozart held that poetry ought to be the obedient child of music. Without a moment's hesitation he proclaims music to reign supreme in the Opera, in which it serves the purpose of illustrating the pervading spirit. In support of this, he reminds us that good music will make us forget even the most wretched libretto—whereas a converse instance can scarcely be adduced—and this unquestionably follows from the *inherent nature of music*. The mere circumstance that it affects our senses more directly and more powerfully than any other art and engrosses them completely, goes to show that the feelings which the words might arouse must needs retire into the background for a time. The music, moreover, through the organ of hearing (in some apparently unaccountable manner) appeals directly to our imagination and our emotional faculty, with a force that temporarily transcends that of the Poetry. (O. Jahn's "Mozart," III., 91.)

controversy to its sources,* will notice in the vast range
from adulation down to ill-breeding all the wit and
smartness of French polemics, but likewise so
childish a treatment of the abstract part of the
question, and such want of deeper knowledge, that
the science of musical æsthetics could gain *nothing*
from the endless disputation. The most gifted con-
troversialists: Suard and the Abbé Arnaud on
Gluck's side, and Marmontel and La Harpe of the
opposite camp, though going repeatedly beyond the
limits of Gluck's critique, and into a more minute
examination of the *dramatic* principle of the Opera,
and its relation to *music*, treated this relation, nevertheless, as one of the many properties of the Opera,
but by no means as one of the most vital importance.
It never struck them that the very life of the Opera
depended on the nature of this relationship. It is
certainly remarkable how very near some of Gluck's
opponents, in particular, were at times to the
position from which the fallacy of the dramatic
principle can be clearly seen and confuted. Thus
La Harpe, in the *Journal de Politique et de Littérature*
of the 5th October, 1777, says : " On objecte qu'il
" n'est pas naturel de chanter un air de cette nature
" dans une situation passionée, que c'est un moyen
" d'arrêter la scène et de nuir à l'effet. Je trouve ces
" objections absolument illusoires. D'abord, dès qu'on
" admet le chant, il faut l'admettre le plus beau possible

---

* The most notable of these polemic writings are to be found in
the collection : " Mémoires pour servir à l'histoire de la Révolution
opérée dans la musique par M. le Chevalier Gluck." (Naples and
Paris, 1781.)

" et il n'est pas plus naturel de chanter mal, que de
" chanter bien. Tous les arts sont fondés sur des
" conventions, sur des données. Quand je viens à
" l'opera, c'est pour entendre la musique. Je n'ignore
" pas, qu' Alceste ne faisait ses Adieux à Admète en
" chantant un air ; mais comme Alceste est sur le
" Théatre pour chanter, si je retrouve sa douleur et
" son amour dans un air bien mélodieux, je jouirai de
" son chant en m'intéressant à son infortune." Is it
credible that La Harpe should have failed to
recognise the security and unassailableness of his
position ? For, after a while, it occurs to him to
object to the duet of *Agamemnon* and *Achilles* in
"Iphigenia" because "it is inconsistent with the
dignity of the two heroes to talk simultaneously."
With this remark he quits the vantage-ground of the
principle of purely *musical* beauty and tacitly—nay,
unconsciously accepts the theory of his adversaries.

The more scrupulous we are in keeping pure the
*dramatic* element of the opera, by withholding from
it the vivifying breath of musical beauty, the more
quickly it faints away like a bird in the exhausted
receiver of an air pump. We have, therefore, no
course open but to fall back upon the pure, *spoken*
drama which, at all events, is a proof of the
*impossibility* of the opera, unless, though fully aware
of the unreality involved, we assign to the *musical*
element the foremost rank. In the true exercise of
the art, this fact has, indeed, never been questioned.
Even Gluck, the most orthodox dramaturgist,
although he originated the fallacy that opera-music
should be nothing but exalted declamation, has, in

practice, often allowed his *musical* genius to get the better of him, and this invariably to the great advantage of the work. The same holds good of Richard Wagner. For the object of these pages, it is enough to emphatically denounce as false Wagner's principal theorem, as stated in the first volume of "Oper und Drama." "The misconception respecting the Opera, "viewed as a work of art, consists in the fact that the "means (the music) is regarded as the end, and the "end (the drama) as the means." An Opera, however, in which the music is really and truly employed *solely as a medium* for dramatic expression is a musical monstrosity.*

---

* I cannot refrain from quoting some very pertinent remarks by Grillparzer and M. Hauptmann :—

Grillparzer calls it "preposterous to make music in the Opera the "mere handmaid of the text" and he goes on to say: "*If music in the "Opera is only there to say over again what the poet has already "expressed, then away with it.* . . . He who knows thy power, "oh melody! which thou, needless of words to explain thy meaning, "bringest down from heaven, thither to return, after stirring the depths "of our soul—he who knows thy charms will never make thee the "humble creature of poetry: to poetry he may, indeed, accord priority "(and I think she has a title to it in the sense in which manhood takes "precedence of youth), but he will acknowledge the existence of thy "own independent realm, and instead of regarding you both in the "light of ruler and subject, or even as guardian and ward, he will deem "you to be sisters." He holds it to be of supreme importance that "no opera be measured by the standard of poetry—for according to "that, every dramatico-musical composition is nonsense—but solely "by the standard of music."

In another passage Grillparzer says: "The opera-composer who is "in the habit of putting his music together mechanically, will find "nothing easier than to adapt his music exactly to the words; whereas "he who aims at making his music an organic whole, with inherent "laws, will constantly come into collision with the words. Every "melody or theme has its own laws of construction and development

One of the inferences to be drawn from Wagner's
proposition (respecting the means and the end) is,
that all composers who have set indifferent librettos

---

" which to the true musical genius are sacred and inviolable, and which
" he dare not infringe in deference to the words.  The musical prosaist
" may, indeed, begin and break off anywhere, for fragments and
" sections can easily be transposed and re-arranged ; but whoever has
" a mind for unity and completeness will give the whole or nothing.
" These remarks must not be construed into a defence of bad librettos,
" they are merely intended as an excuse and a palliation.  It is for this
" reason that Rossini's shallow trifling is superior to Mosel's intellec-
" tual parrotry which destroys the very essence of music, in order to
" stumble along the line already traced by the poet.  For this reason
" again, many incongruities may be shown to exist in Mozart's Operas,
" but none in Gluck's.  Lastly, for this reason the much-admired
" characteristic of music is often but an extremely negative merit, joy
" being generally expressed by not-sadness ; sorrow by not-gladness ;
" gentleness by not-harshness; rage by not-gentleness; love by means
" of flutes, and despair with trumpets, kettle-drums, and double-basses.
" The composer ought to be guided by the *incidents* as they arise, not by
" the *words*, and if his music is more eloquent he may rightly disregard
" the libretto."  Do not many of these aphorisms, written so many
years ago, sound like a condemnation of Wagner's theories and the
Walkyrs-style ?  Grillparzer displays a profound knowledge of the
nature of the public, when he says : " Those, who in the *Opera* look
" for *purely dramatic* effects, are, as a rule, those who expect *musical*
" effects from *dramatic* poetry—in other words, an effect without a
" cause."  (IX., 144.)

M. Hauptmann, in his letters to O. Jahn, follows a similar line of
thought : " It seemed to me (on hearing Gluck's operas) as if the com-
" poser was bent, above all, on being true ; not *musically true*, but *true* in
" respect of the *words*.  This is frequently the high road to musical
" failure, for, whereas speech may be abruptly broken off, music ought
" to slowly die away.  Music will ever remain the vowel, in respect of
" which the word is but the consonant and here, as always, it is the
" vowel which plays the principal part, as being the essential and not
" the auxiliary sound.  The music invariably stands out in strong
" relief, how well soever it may fit the words, and it ought always to
" be worth listening to for its own sake."  (" Briefe an Spohr," &c.,
edited by F. Hiller, Leipzig, 1876, page 106.)

to anything better than indifferent music, were
guilty of a great impropriety, as we ourselves are in
admiring such music.

The connection of poetry with music and with the
opera is a sort of morganatic union, and the more
closely we examine this morganatic union of musical
beauty and definite thoughts, the more sceptical do
we become as regards its indissolubility.

How is it that in every song slight alterations may
be introduced, which, without in the least detracting
from the accuracy of expression, immediately destroy
the beauty of the theme? This would be impossible,
if the latter were inseparably connected with the
former. How, again, is it, that many a song, though
adequately expressing the drift of the poem, is nevertheless quite intolerable? The theory that music
is capable of expressing emotions, furnishes us with
no explanation. In what, then, consists the
beautiful in music, if it does not consist in the
emotional element?

An altogether different and independent element
remains, which we shall presently examine more
closely.

E

## CHAPTER III.

So far we have considered only the negative aspect of the question, and have sought to expose the fallacy that the beautiful in music depends upon the accurate expression of feelings.

We must now, by way of completing the exposition, bring into light also its positive aspect, and endeavour to determine of what nature the beautiful in music is.

*Its nature is specifically musical.* By this we mean that the beautiful is not contingent upon, or in need of any subject introduced from without, but that it consists wholly of sounds artistically combined. The ingenious co-ordination of intrinsically pleasing sounds, their consonance and contrast, their flight and re-approach, their increasing and diminishing strength—this it is, which in free and unimpeded forms, presents itself to our mental vision.

The primordial element of music is *euphony*, and *rhythm* is its soul. Rhythm in general, or the harmony of a symmetrical structure ; and rhythm in particular, or the systematically reciprocal motion of its several parts within a given measure. The crude material which the composer has to fashion, the vast profusion of which it is impossible to fully estimate, is the entire scale of *musical notes* and their inherent adaptability to an endless variety of

melodies, harmonies, and rhythms. *Melody*, unex-
hausted, nay, inexhaustible, is pre-eminently the
source of musical beauty. *Harmony* with its countless
modes of transforming, inverting, and intensifying,
offers the material for constantly new developments ;
while *rhythm*, the main artery of the musical
organism, is the regulator of both, and enhances the
charms of the " timbre " in its rich varieties.

To the question—what is to be expressed with all
this material? the answer will be : *musical ideas*.
Now, a musical idea, reproduced in its entirety, is
not only an object of intrinsic beauty, but also an
end in itself, and not a means for representing
feelings and thoughts.

The essence of music is *sound and motion*.

*The arabesque*, a branch of the art of ornamenta-
tion, dimly betokens in what manner music may
exhibit *forms of beauty*, though no definite emotion
be involved. We see a plexus of flourishes, now
bending into graceful curves, now rising in bold
sweeps ; moving now towards, and now away from
each other ; correspondingly matched in small and
large arcs ; apparently incommensurable, yet duly
proportioned throughout ; with a duplicate or
counterpart to every segment ; in fine, a compound
of oddments, and yet a perfect whole. Imagine
now an arabesque, not still and motionless, but
rising before our eyes in constantly changing forms.
Behold the broad and delicate lines, how they
pursue one another ; how from a gentle curve they
rise up into lofty heights, presently to descend
again ; how they widen and contract ; surprising

E 2

the eye with a marvellous alternation of quiescence
and mobility.  The image thus becomes nobler and
more exalted.  If, moreover, we conceive this living
arabesque as the active emanation of inventive
genius, the artistic fulness of whose imagination is
incessantly flowing into the heart of these moving
forms, the effect, we think, will be not unlike that
of *music*.

When young, we have probably all been delighted
with the ever-changing tints and forms of a
*kaleidoscope*.  Now, music is a kind of kaleidoscope,
though its forms can be appreciated only by an
infinitely higher ideation.  It brings forth a profuse-
ness of beautiful tints and forms, now sharply con-
trasted and now almost imperceptibly graduated; all
logically connected with each other, yet all novel
in their effect, forming, as it were, a complete and
self-subsistent whole, free from any alien admixture.
The main difference consists in the fact that the
*musical kaleidoscope* is the direct product of a creative
mind, whereas the optic one is but a cleverly constructed mechanical toy.  If, however, we stepped
beyond the bounds of analogy, and in real earnest
attempted to raise mere colour to the rank of music
by foisting on one art the means of another, we
should be landed in the region of such puerile
contrivances as the "Colour Piano" or the "Ocular
Organ," though these contrivances significantly
prove both phenomena to have, morphologically, a
common root.

If any sentimental lover of music thinks that
analogies, such as the one mentioned, are degrading

to the art, we reply that the only question is whether
they are *relevant* or not.    A subject is not degraded
by being studied.    If we wish to disregard the
attributes of motion and successive formation, which
render a comparison with the kaleidoscope particularly applicable, we may, forsooth, find a more
dignified parallel for beautiful music in architecture, the human body, or a landscape, because these
all possess original beauty of outline and colour, quite
irrespective of the intellectual substratum, the soul.

The reason why people have failed to discover the
beauties in which pure music abounds, is, in great
measure, to be found in the *underrating*, by the older
systems of æsthetics, of the *sensuous element*, and in its
subordination to morality and feeling—in Hegel to
the "idea."    Every art sets out from the sensuous
and operates within its limits.    The theory relating
to the expression of feelings ignores this fact, and
disdainfully pushing aside the act of *hearing*, it passes
on immediately to the *feelings*.    Music, say they, is
food for the soul, and the organ of hearing is beneath
their notice.

True, it is not for the organ of hearing as such, for
the "labyrinth" or the "tympanum" that a
Beethoven composes.    But our *imagination*, which is
so constituted as to be affected by auditory impressions
(and in relation to which the term *organ* means
something very different from a channel directed
towards the world of physical phenomena), delights
in the sounding forms and musical structures,
and, conscious of their sensuous nature, lives in the
immediate and free contemplation of the beautiful.

It is extremely difficult to define this self-subsistent and specifically musical beauty. As music has no prototype in nature, and expresses no definite conceptions, we are compelled to speak of it either in dry, technical terms, or in the language of poetic fiction. Its kingdom is, indeed, " not of this world." All the fantastic descriptions, characterizations, and periphrases are either metaphorical or false. What in any other art is still descriptive, is in music already figurative. Of music it is impossible to form any but a musical conception, and it can be comprehended and enjoyed only in and for itself.

The "specifically musical" must not, however, be understood only in the sense of acoustic beauty or symmetry of parts—both of which elements it embraces as of secondary importance—and still less can we speak of "a display of sounds to tickle the ear," or use similar phraseology, which is generally intended to emphasize the absence of an intellectual principle. But, by laying stress on musical beauty, we do not exclude the intellectual principle; on the contrary, we imply it as essential ; for we would not apply the term " beautiful " to anything wanting in intellectual beauty; and in tracing the essential nature of beauty to a morphological source, we wish it to be understood that the intellectual element is most intimately connected with these sonorific forms. The term "form " in musical language is peculiarly significant. The forms created by *sound* are not empty; not the envelope enclosing a vacuum, but a well, replete with the living creation of inventive genius. Music, then, as compared with the arabesque, is a *picture*, yet a picture the subject of which we cannot define in words, or include in any category of thought. In music there is both meaning and logical sequence, but in a *musical* sense; it is a language we speak and understand, but which we are unable to *translate.* It is a highly suggestive fact that, in speaking of musical compositions, we likewise employ the term "thought," and a critical mind easily distinguishes real thoughts from hollow phrases, precisely as in speech. The Germans significantly use the term "Satz" (sentence) for the logical consummation of a part of a composition, for we know exactly when it is finished, just as in the case of a written or spoken sentence, though each has a logic of its own.

The logic in music, which produces in us a feeling of satisfaction, rests on certain elementary laws of nature, which govern both the human organism and the phenomena of sound. It is, above all, the primordial law of "harmonic progression" which, similarly to the curve-lines in painting and sculpture, contains the germ of development in its main forms, and the—unfortunately almost unexplained—cause of the link which connects the various musical phenomena.

All musical elements are in some occult manner connected with each other by certain natural affinities, and since rhythm, melody, and harmony are under their invisible sway, the music created by man must conform to them—any combinations conflicting with them bearing the impress of caprice and ugliness. Though not demonstrable with scientific precision, these affinities are instinctively felt by every experienced ear, and the organic completeness and logic, or the absurdity and unnaturalness of a group of sounds, are intuitively known, without the intervention of a definite conception as the standard of measure, the *tertium comparationis.**

From this negative rationalness, inherent in music and founded on laws of nature, springs the possibility of its becoming invested also with *positive* forms of beauty.

The act of composing is a mental working on material capable of receiving the forms which the mind intends to give. The musical material in the hands of creative genius is as plastic and pliable as it is profuse. Unlike the architect, who has to mould the coarse and unwieldy rock, the composer reckons with the ulterior effect of past sounds. More ethereal and subtle than the material of any other art, sound adapts itself with great facility to any idea the composer may have in his mind. Now, as the union of sounds (from the interdependence of which the beautiful in music flows) is not effected

---

* " Poetry may utilise the ugly (the unbeautiful) even in a fairly "liberal measure, for, as it affects the feelings only through the " medium of the ideas which it directly suggests, the knowledge that " it is a means adapted to an end will, from the outset, soften its " impression, even to the extent of creating a most profound sensation, " by force of contrast and by stimulating the imagination. The effect " of music, however, is perceived and assimilated directly by the " senses, and the verdict of the intellect comes too late to correct the " disturbing factor of ugliness. It is for this reason that Shakespeare " was justified in making use of the horrible, while Mozart was obliged " to remain within the limits of the beautiful." (Grillparzer IX., 142.)

by mechanically stringing them together, but by acts of a free imagination, the intellectual force and idiosyncrasy of the particular mind will give to every composition its *individual character*. A musical composition, as the creation of a thinking and feeling mind, may, therefore, itself possess intellectuality and pathos in a high degree. Every musical work ought to bear this stamp of intellectuality, but the *music itself* must furnish evidence of its existence. Our opinion regarding the seat of the intellectual and emotional elements of a musical composition stands in the same relation to the popular way of thinking as the idea of *immanence* does to that of *transcendence*. The object of every art is to clothe in some material form an idea which has originated in the artist's imagination. In music this idea is an *acoustic* one; it cannot be expressed in words and subsequently translated into sounds. The initial force of a composition is the invention of some definite theme, and not the desire to describe a given emotion by musical means. Thanks to that primitive and mysterious power, whose mode of action will for ever be hidden from us, a theme, a melody flashes on the composer's mind. The origin of this *first* germ cannot be explained, but must simply be accepted as a fact. When once it has taken root in the composer's imagination, it forthwith begins to grow and develop; the principal theme being the centre round which the branches group themselves in all conceivable ways, though always unmistakably related to it. The beauty of an independent and simple theme appeals to our æsthetic feeling with that directness, which tolerates no explanation, except, perhaps, that of its inherent fitness and the harmony of parts, to the exclusion of any alien factor. It pleases for its own sake, like an arabesque, a column, or some spontaneous product of nature—a leaf or a flower.

There is no greater and more frequent error than to distinguish between "beautiful music," *with* and *without* a definite subject. The error is due to the extremely narrow conception of the beautiful in music, leading people to regard the artistically constructed form and the soul infused into it, as two independent and unrelated existences. All compositions are accordingly divided into full and empty "champagne bottles"; musical "champagne," however, has the peculiarity of developing *with* the bottle.

One musical thought is refined in and through itself and for no further reason ; another is vulgar ; this final cadence is imposing, while by the alteration of but two notes it becomes commonplace. (We are perfectly justified in calling a musical theme grand, graceful, warm, hollow, vulgar ; but all these terms are exclusively suggestive of the *musical* character of the particular passage. To define the musical complexion of a given theme, we often speak in terms used to describe *emotions*, such as "proud, gloomy, tender, ardent, longing." But we may with equal justice select them from a different order of phenomena, and call a piece of music, "sweet, fresh, cloudy, cold." Our feelings, to be descriptive of the character of a musical composition, must be regarded in the light of mere *phenomena*, just as any other phenomenon which happens to present certain analogies. Epithets, such as we have mentioned, may be used so long as we remain fully conscious of their figurative sense— nay, we may even be unable to avoid them ; but let us never say, this piece of music *expresses* pride, &c. A close examination of the musical definiteness of a theme convinces us however—the inscrutability of the ultimate ontological causes notwithstanding— that there are various proximate causes with which the intellectual element in a composition is intimately associated. Every musical factor (such as an interval, the "timbre," a chord, the rhythm, &c.) has a distinctive feature of its own and its individual mode of action. Though the composer's mind be a mystery, its product is quite within the grasp of our understanding.

A theme, harmonised with the common chord, sounds differently if harmonised with the chord of the sixth; a melody progressing by an interval of the seventh produces quite a distinct effect from one progressing by an interval of the sixth. The rhythm, the volume of sound, or the "timbre"—each alters the specific character of a theme entirely—in fine, every single musical factor necessarily contributes to a certain passage assuming just *this* particular aspect, and affecting the listener in *this* particular way. What it is that makes Halévy's music appear fantastic, that of Auber graceful—what enables us immediately to recognise Mendelssohn or Spohr— all this may be traced to purely *musical* causes, without having recourse to the mysterious element of the *feelings*.

On the other hand, *why* the frequent chords of $\frac{6}{4}$ and the concise, diatonic themes of Mendelssohn, the chromatic and enharmonic music of Spohr, the short two-bar rhythm of Auber, &c., invariably produce this specific impression and none other—this enigma, it is true, neither psychology nor physiology can solve.

If, however, we enquire into the *proximate* cause—and that is, after all, what concerns us most in any art—we shall find that the thrilling effect of a theme is owing, not to the supposed extreme grief of the composer, but to the extreme intervals ; not to the beating of his heart, but to the beating of the drums ; not to the craving of his soul, but to the chromatic progression of the music. The *link* connecting the two we would by no means ignore ; on the contrary, we shall presently subject it to a careful analysis. Meanwhile, we must remember that a scientific enquiry into the effect of a theme can deal only with such *musical* factors as have an enduring and objective existence, and not with the presumable state of mind in which the composer happened to be. The conclusion reached by arguing from the composer's state of mind directly to the effect of the music *might*, perchance, be correct ; but the most important part of the syllogism, the middle term—*i.e.*, *the music itself*, would thus be ignored.

A good composer always has, perhaps more by intuition than by rote, a *practical* knowledge of the character of every musical element ; but in order

to give a rationale of the various musical sensations
and impressions, we require a *theoretical* knowledge
of those characters from the most intricate combinations down to scarcely distinguishable gradations.
The specific effect of a melody must not be taken as
"a marvel mysterious and unaccountable," which
we can only "feel" or "divine"; but it is the
inevitable result of the musical factors united in this
particular manner. A short or long rhythm, a
diatonic or chromatic progression—each has its
individual physiognomy and an effect of its own. An
intelligent musician will, therefore, get a much
clearer notion of the character of a composition
which he has not heard himself, by being told that it
contains, for instance, too many diminished sevenths,
or too many tremolos, than by the most poetic
description of the emotional crises through which
the listener passed.

To ascertain the nature of each musical factor,
its connection with a specific effect—its proximate,
not its ultimate cause—and finally, to explain these
particular observations by more general laws would
be to establish that "philosophic foundation of
music" to which so many writers aspire, though
none has ever told us in which sense he understands
this phrase. The psychical or physical effect of a
chord, a rhythm, or an interval is not accounted for
by saying that *this* is the expression of hope, *that* the
expression of disappointment, as we should say, this
is red, that green, but only by placing specifically
musical attributes in general æsthetic categories,
and the latter under one supreme principle. After

having explained the isolated action of each single
element, it would be incumbent upon us to show
in what manner they govern and modify one another
in all their various combinations. Most musical
critics have ascribed the intellectual merit of a
composition more particularly to the *harmony* and the
*contrapuntal* accompaniment. The arguments, however, are both superficial and desultory. *Melody*, the
alleged vehicle of sensuousness and emotion, was attributed to the inspiration of genius—the Italian school
accordingly receiving a gracious word of praise ; while
*harmony*, the supposed vehicle of sterling thought, in
contradistinction to melody, was deemed to be simply
the result of study and reflection. It is strange how
long people were satisfied with so unscientific a view
of the subject. Both propositions contain a grain
of truth, but they are neither universally applicable
nor are the two factors in question, in reality, ever so
strictly isolated. The soul and the talent for musical
construction are bound up in one inseparable whole.
Melody and harmony issue simultaneously in *one and
the same* armour from the composer's mind. Neither
the principle of subordination nor that of contrast
affect the *nature* of the relation of harmony to melody.
Both may display now an equal force of independent
development, and now an equally strong tendency
to voluntary subordination—yet, in either case,
supreme intellectual beauty may be attained. Is it,
perchance, the (altogether absent) *harmony* in the
principal themes of Beethoven's Overture to
"Coriolanus," or of Mendelssohn's Overture to
" The Hebrides," which gives them the character of

profound thought? Is the intellectual merit of
Rossini's theme "Oh, Matilda!" or of some
Neapolitan song, likely to be enhanced by sub-
stituting for the original meagre harmony a *basso
continuo*, or some complicated succession of chords?
The theme was conceived with *that* harmony, *that*
rhythm, and *that* instrumentation. The intellectual
merit lies in the union of *all* these factors; hence the
mutilation of one entails that of the others. The
*prominence* of the melody, the rhythm, or the
harmony, as the case may be, improves the effect of
the whole, and it is sheer pedantry to say that the
excellence or the triviality is owing here to the
presence of certain chords, and there to their
absence. The camellia is destitute of odour, and the
lily of colour; the rose is rich both in odour and
colour; each is beautiful, and yet their respective
attributes cannot be interchanged.

A "philosophic foundation of music" would first
of all require us, then, to determine the definite
conceptions which are invariably connected with each
musical element and the nature of this connection.
The double requirement of a strictly scientific framework, and an extremely comprehensive casuistry,
renders it a most arduous though not an impossible
task, unless, indeed, our ideal is that of a science of
music in the sense in which chemistry and
physiology are sciences!

The manner in which the creative act takes place
in the mind of a composer of instrumental music
gives us a very clear insight into the peculiar nature
of musical beauty. A *musical* idea originates in the

composer's imagination; he develops it — more
and more crystals coalesce with it, until by
imperceptible degrees the whole structure in its main
features appears before him. Nothing then remains
to be done. but to examine the composition, to
regulate its rhythm and modify it according to
the canons of the art. The composer of instrumental music never thinks of representing a definite
subject·; otherwise he would be placed in a false
position, rather outside than within the domain
of music. His composition in such a case
would be *programme music*, unintelligible without
the programme. If this brings the name of Berlioz
to our mind, we do not hereby call into question
or underrate his brilliant talent. In his step
followed Liszt, with his much weaker " Symphonic
Poems."

As the same block of marble is converted by one
sculptor into the most exquisite forms, by another
into a clumsy botch, so the musical scale, by
different manipulation, becomes now an Overture of
Beethoven, and now one of Verdi. In what respect
do they differ? Is it that one of them expresses
more exalted feelings, or the same feelings more
accurately? No, but simply because its musical
structure is more beautiful. One piece of music is
good, another bad, because one composer invents a
theme full of life, another a commonplace one;
because the former elaborates his music with
ingenious originality, whereas with the latter it
becomes, if anything, worse and worse; because the
harmony in one case is varied and novel, whereas

in the other it drags on miserably in its poverty ; because in one the rhythm is like a pulse, full of strength and vitality, whereas in the other it is not unlike a tattoo. There is no art which, like music, uses up so quickly such a variety of forms. Modulations, cadences, intervals and harmonious progressions become so hackneyed within fifty, nay, thirty years, that a truly original composer cannot well employ them any longer, and is thus compelled to think of a new musical phraseology. Of a great number of compositions which rose far above the trivialities of their day, it would be quite correct to say that there *was* a time when they were beautiful. Among the occult and primitive affinities of the musical elements and the myriads of possible combinations, a great composer will discover the most subtle and un-apparent ones. He will call into being forms of music which seemingly are conceived at the com-poser's pure caprice, and yet, for some mysterious and unaccountable reason, stand to each other in the relation of cause and effect. Such compositions in their entirety, or fragments of them, may, without hesitation, be said to contain the " spark of genius." This shows how mistaken Oulibicheff is, when he asserts, that instrumental music cannot possibly be "*spirituel*," because the "*esprit*" of the composer consists solely in *adapting* his music in " a certain manner to a direct or indirect programme." In our opinion we are quite warranted in saying, that the celebrated D sharp in the *Allegro*, or the descending " unisono " passage in the Overture to " Don

F

Giovanni," is imbued with the spirit of genius. The former, however, as little represents (as Oulibicheff imagines) "*Don Giovanni's* hostile attitude to the human race," as the latter does "the parents, the husbands, the brothers and the lovers of the women whom *Don Giovanni* seduced." Such interpretations are not only questionable in themselves, but are particularly so in respect of Mozart, who—the greatest musical genius the world has ever seen — transformed into music all he touched. Oulibicheff also thinks that Mozart's G minor Symphony accurately describes the history of a passionate amour in four different phases. But the G minor Symphony is music, neither more nor less ; and that is quite enough. If instead of looking for the expression of definite states of mind, or certain events in musical works, we seek *music* only, we shall then, free from other associations, enjoy the perfections it so abundantly affords. Wherever musical beauty is wanting, no meaning, however profound, which sophistical subtlety may read into the work can ever compensate for it ; and where it exists, the meaning is a matter of indifference. It directs our musical judgment, at all events, into a wrong channel. The same people who regard music as a mode in which the human intellect finds expression—which it neither is nor ever can be, on account of its inability to impart *convictions*—these very people have also brought the word "intention" into vogue. But in music there is no "intention" that can make up for "invention." Whatever is not clearly contained in the music, is to all intents and purposes non-existent, and what it does contain has passed the stage of mere intention. The saying: "He intends something" is generally used in a eulogistic sense. To us it seems rather to imply an unfavourable criticism which, translated into plain language would run thus : the composer would like to produce something, but he cannot. Now, an *art* is *to do* something, and he who cannot do anything takes refuge in—" intentions."

As the musical elements of a composition are the source of its beauty, so are they likewise the source of the laws of its construction. A great number of false and confused notions are entertained on this subject, but we will only single out one.

We mean the commonly accepted theory of the *Sonata* and *Symphony*, grounded on the assumption that feelings are expressible by musical means. In accordance with this theory, the task of the composer is to represent in the several parts of the Sonata four *states of mind*, all differing among themselves, and yet related to one another. (How ?) In order to account for the connection which undoubtedly exists between the various parts, and to explain the difference in their effect, it is naïvely taken for granted that a definite feeling underlies each of them. The construction put upon them sometimes fits, but more frequently it does not, and it never follows as a necessary consequence. It will always, however, be a matter of course, that the four different parts are bound up in a harmonious whole, and that each should set off and heighten the effect of the others, according to the æsthetic laws of *music*. We are indebted to the inventive genius of M. v. Schwindt for a very interesting illustration of Beethoven's "Fantasia for the Pianoforte" (Op. 80), the several parts of which the artist interprets as representing connected incidents in the lives of the principal actors, and then gives a pictorial description of them. Now, just as the painter transforms the sounds into scenes and shapes, so does the listener transform them into feelings and occurrences. Both stand in a certain relation to the music, but neither of them in a *necessary* one, and it is only with *necessary* relations that science is concerned.

It is often alleged that Beethoven, when making the rough sketch of a composition, had before him certain incidents or states of mind. Whenever Beethoven (or any other composer) adopted this method, he did so to smooth his task ; to render the achievement of musical unity easier by keeping in view the connecting links of certain objective phenomena. If Berlioz, Liszt, and others fancied that a poem, a title, or an event yielded them something *more* than that, they were labouring under a delusion. It is the *frame of mind* bent on *musical unity* which gives to the four parts of a sonata the character of an organically-related whole, and not their connection with an *object* which the composer may have in view. Where the latter denied himself the luxury of these poetic leading-strings, and followed purely musical inspiration, we shall find no other than a musical unity of parts. Æsthetically speaking, it is utterly indifferent whether Beethoven really did associate all his works with certain ideas.

We do not know them, and as far as the composition is concerned, they do not exist. It is the composition itself, apart from all comment, which has to be judged ; and as the lawyer completely ignores whatever is not in his brief, so æsthetic criticism must disregard whatever lies outside the work of art. If the several parts of a composition bear the stamp of unity, their correlation must have its root in musical principles.*

---

* Beethoven-oracles like Mr. Lobe and others were greatly scandalized at these remarks. By way of replying, we cannot do better than quote Otto Jahn's views in his essay on the new edition of Beethoven's works published by Breitkopf and Härtel (" Gesammelte Aufsätze über Musik "), which fully confirm our own opinions. Citing Schindler's well-known anecdote that, when asked as to the meaning of his D minor and F minor Sonatas, Beethoven replied : " Read Shakespeare's ' Tempest,' " Jahn goes on to say, that the querist, after having read the play, will doubtless become convinced that Shakespeare's " Tempest" did not affect him in the same manner as it did Beethoven, and that it failed to inspire him with D minor and F minor Sonatas. That just this play should have suggested to Beethoven those musical marvels is certainly an interesting fact; but the attempt to understand them by the light of Shakespeare would be a proof of a somewhat beclouded musical judgment. When composing the Adagio of his F major Quartet (Op. 18, No. 1) Beethoven is said to have had the grave-scene in " Romeo and Juliet " in his mind. Now, if one were to carefully read the scene and keep it in his mind's eye, while listening to the music, would this enhance or spoil the enjoyment of the composition ? Titles and foot-notes, even authentic ones by Beethoven himself, are not calculated to lead to a clearer apprehension of the spirit and drift of the work. On the contrary, such factors are apt to give rise to fallacies and misconceptions, as some of Beethoven's titles have actually done. It is a well-known fact that the charming Sonata in E flat major (Op. 81) bears the following inscription : " Les adieux, l'absence, le retour," and being thought a reliable instance of programme-music, it is interpreted with every confidence. " That " they are incidents in the life of a loving couple," says Marx, who

To avoid even the possibility of misapprehension, we will now define our conception of the "beautiful in music" from three points of view. The "beautiful in music," in the specific sense in which we understand it, is neither confined to the "classical style," nor does it imply a preference for this over the "romantic style." It may exist in one style no less than the other, and may occur in Bach as well as in Beethoven; in Mozart as well as in Schumann. Our proposition is thus above all suspicion of partisanship. The whole course of the present enquiry never approaches the question of what *ought to be*, but simply of what *is*. We can deduce from it no definite ideal of the truly beautiful in music, but it enables us to show what is equally beautiful even in the most opposite styles.

Not long since the fashion began to regard works of art in connection with the ideas and events of the

---

leaves it, however, an open question whether the lovers are married or not, "was, of course, to be presumed; but the music itself contains the *proof* of it." "The lovers spread out their arms as "migratory birds do their wings," says Lenz, with reference to the concluding passages of the Sonata. Now it so happens that Beethoven wrote on the original of the first part: "The farewell on "the occasion of his Imperial Highness, the *Archduke Rudolf's* "departure, the 4th May, 1809," and on the title-page of the second part: "The arrival of his Imperial Highness the *Archduke Rudolf*, "the 30th of January, 1810." How he would have ridiculed the imputation that he desired to impersonate towards the Archduke "the "female flapping her wings and dying with bliss and fond caresses." "It is, therefore, a matter for congratulation," Jahn remarks in conclusion, "that Beethoven (as a rule) refrained from uttering words "calculated to beguile people into the belief that he who understands "the title, understands also the composition. His *music says all he* "*wished to say*."

time which gave them birth. This connection is undeniable and exists probably also in music. Being a product of the human mind, it must naturally bear some relation to the other products of mind ; to contemporaneous works of poetry and the fine arts ; to the state of society, literature, and the sciences of the period ; and finally, to the individual experiences and convictions of the author. To observe and demonstrate the existence of this connection in the case of certain composers and works is not only a justifiable proceeding, but also a true gain to knowledge. We should, nevertheless, always remember, that parallelisms between specific works of art and the events of certain epochs belong to the *history of art* rather than to the *science of æsthetics*. Though methodological considerations may render it necessary to connect the history of art with the science of æsthetics, it is yet of the utmost importance that the proper domain of each of these sciences be rigourously guarded from encroachment on either side. The historian viewing a work of art in all its bearings may discover in Spontini " the expression of French imperialism," in Rossini "the political restoration "; but the student of æsthetics must restrict himself to the examination of the works themselves, in order to determine what is beautiful in them and why it is so. The æsthetic enquirer knows nothing (nor can he be expected to know anything) about the personal circumstances or the political surroundings of the composer—he hears and believes nothing, but what the music itself contains. He will, therefore, without knowing the

name or the biography of the author, detect in
Beethoven's Symphonies impetuousness and strug-
gling, an unsatisfied longing and a defiance, suppor-
ted by a consciousness of strength. But he could
never glean from his works that he favoured re-
publicanism, that he was a bachelor and deaf, or
any of the numerous circumstances on which the
art-historian is wont to dilate ; nor could such facts
enhance the merit of the music. It may be very
interesting and praiseworthy to compare the various
schools of philosophy to which Bach, Mozart, and
Haydn belonged, and to draw a parallel between them
and the works of these composers. It is, however, a
most arduous undertaking, and one which can but
open the door to fallacies in proportion as it attempts
to establish causal relations. The danger of exagger-
ation is exceedingly great, when once this principle
is accepted. The slender influence of contemporari-
ness may easily be construed as an inherent necessity,
and the ever-untranslatable language of music be
interpreted in the way which best fits the particular
theory : all depends on the reasoning abilities ;
the same paradox which in the mouth of an
accomplished dialectician appears a truism, seems
the greatest nonsense in the mouth of an unskilled
speaker.

Hegel, too, by his dissertation on music, has been
the cause of misconceptions, for he quite unconsciously confounded the point of view of *art-history*,
which was pre-eminently his own, with that of pure
æsthetics, and attributed an explicitness to music
which, as such, it never possessed. The character

of a piece of music undoubtedly stands in some relation to the character of its author; but for the student of æsthetics the relation is non-existent. The abstract notion of a necessary interdependence of *all* phenomena whatsoever may in its concrete application be distorted into a caricature of the reality. It requires, now-a-days, great moral courage to militate against a doctrine which is advocated with such skill and eloquence, and to openly affirm that " the grasp of historical relations" is one thing, and "æsthetic judgment" another.* Objectively speaking, it is beyond doubt, *firstly,* that the different styles of expression of distinct works and schools are due to a completely different collocation of the *musical* elements; and *secondly,* that, what rightly gives pleasure in a composition, be it a severely classical Fugue of Bach, or the dreamiest Nocturne of Chopin, is the beautiful in a *musical* sense only.

Even less than with the classical does the beautiful in music coincide with one of its branches, the *architectonic.* The rigid sublimity of super-incumbent harmonies, and the artistic blending of the many different parts (of which no isolated segment is ever free and self-dependent, because the complete work alone is so) have their imprescriptible justification; yet those imposing and sombre pyramids of sound of the old Italian and Dutch

---

* If we refer here to Riehl's " Musikalische Characterköpfe," we do so in grateful acknowledgment of the intellectual enjoyment to be derived from the book.

schools, and the finely-chased salt-cellars and silver candlesticks, so to speak, of venerable Sebastian Bach, are but small provinces within the kingdom of musical beauty.

Many schools of æsthetics think musical enjoyment is fully accounted for by the pleasure derived from mere *regularity* and *symmetry;* but these never were the sole attributes of beauty in the abstract, and much less so of beauty in music. The most insipid theme may be symmetrical. "Symmetry" connotes proportion only, and leaves unanswered the question: *what* it is that impresses us as being symmetrical? A systematic distribution of parts, both uninteresting and commonplace, often exists in the most pitiable compositions, but the musical sense wants symmetry combined with *originality.**

---

* To illustrate this proposition, I make free in quoting the following passage from my work " Die moderne Oper " (Preface, page vi.) :—

" The celebrated saying that the 'truly beautiful' (who, by the " way, is to be the judge of this attribute?) can never lose its charms, " even after the greatest lapse of time, is, as far as music is concerned, " little more than an empty, though pompous phrase. Music proceeds " on the lines of Nature, which every autumn allows a world of flowers " to moulder into dust, whence new blossoms arise. Musical com- " positions being the work of man, the product of a certain in- " dividuality, period, or state of civilization, invariably contain the " germs of slow or rapid decay. Among the great forms of music, the " opera is the most composite and conventional, and, therefore, the " most transient form. It may sadden us to reflect that even com- " paratively new operas of a lofty and brilliant order (Spohr, Spontini) " have already begun to disappear from the stage. The fact is, never- " theless, beyond dispute, nor can the process be stayed by invectives " against the evil ' spirit of the time '—so characteristic of all ages. " Time, forsooth, is a spirit, but a spirit which creates its own body. " The theatre is the forum for the living aspirations of the public, as

Oerstedt, to crown all, carried this Platonic doctrine so far as to cite the circle, for which he claims
positive beauty, as a parallel case.   Should he, himself, never have experienced the horror of a completely
round composition ?

From caution, rather than from necessity, we may
add, that the beautiful in music is totally independent of *mathematics*.   Amateurs (among whom there
are also some sentimental authors) have a singularly
vague notion of the part played by mathematics in
the composition of music.   Not content with the
fact that the vibrations of sound, the intervals and
the phenomena of consonance and dissonance, rest
on mathematical principles, they feel convinced that
the *beautiful* in a composition may likewise be reduced to numbers.   The study of harmony and the
counterpoint is looked upon as a kind of Cabala,

---

" distinguished from the quiet study of the reader of musical scores.
" The stage is the life of the drama; the fight for its possession is the
" drama's struggle for existence.  In this battle an inferior work often
" triumphs over its superior predecessors, if it breathes the spirit of the
" time and if its pulse throbs in harmony with *our* feelings and desires.
" Both the artist and the public have a justifiable longing for something
" new in Music, and those critics whose admiration is restricted to
" older music and who lack the courage to do homage also to modern
" compositions undermine the productive power of art.  The delightful
" belief in the imperishableness of music, must, of course, be given up.
" Has not every age proclaimed with the same ungrounded assurance
" the undying beauty of *its* best operas ?  How long is it since Adam
' Hiller of Leipzig declared, that if Hasse's Operas should ever fail to
' charm an audience, a state of universal depravity would ensue ?
" How long is it since Schubart, the musical æsthetic of Hohenasperg,
" pronounced it wholly inconceivable that the composer Jomelli could
" ever sink into oblivion ?  And what are Hasse and Jomelli to us at
" the present day ? "

teaching the "calculus," as it were, of musical composition.

Mathematics, though furnishing an indispensable key to the study of the physical aspect of music, must not be overrated, as regards its value in the finished composition. No mathematical calculation ever enters into a composition, be it the best or the worst. Creations of inventive genius are not arithmetical sums. Experiments with the monochord, the figures producible by sonorous vibrations, the mathematical ratios of musical intervals, &c., lie all outside the domain of *æsthetics*, which begins only where those elementary relations cease to be of importance. Mathematics merely controls the intellectual manipulation of the primary elements of music, and is secretly at work in the most simple relations. The musical thought, however, originates without the aid of mathematics. What Oerstedt means, by enquiring whether the lifetime of several " mathematicians would suffice to calculate all the " beauties in *one* Symphony by Mozart "* we, for our part, are at a loss to understand. *What* is to be, or can be calculated ? Is it the number of vibrations of each note as compared with the next, or the relative lengths of the divisions and sub-divisions of the composition? That which raises a series of musical sounds into the region of music proper and above the range of physical experiments is something free from external constraint, a spiritualised,

---

* " Geist in der Natur," Volume III., translated into German by Kannegiesser. Page 32.

and, therefore, incalculable something. Mathematics has as little and as much to do with musical compositions, as such, as with the generative processes of the other arts; for mathematics must, after all, guide also the hand of the painter and sculptor : it is the rhythmical principle of verse; it regulates the work of the architect and the figures of the dancer. Though in all accurate knowledge, mathematics must have a place, we should never attribute to it a positive and creative power, as some musicians, the conservatives in the science of æsthetics, would fain have us do. Mathematics and the excitation of feelings are in a similar position—they have a place in all arts, but in no art is there so much stress laid upon them as in music.

Between *language* and music, parallels have also been frequently drawn and an attempt made to lay down for the latter laws governing only the former. The relation between *song* and language is patent enough, no matter whether we found it on the identity of the physiological conditions, or on the character which both have in common—namely, that of expressing thoughts and feelings by means of the human voice. The analogy, indeed, is so obvious as to render unnecessary further discussion. We admit at once that wherever music is merely the subjective manifestation of a state of mind, the laws of *speech* are, in a measure, applicable also to *singing*. That under the influence of passion the pitch of the voice is raised, while the propitiating orator lowers it; that sentences of great force are spoken slowly, and unimportant ones quickly; these and kindred facts the composer of songs, and the *musical dramatist* especially, will ever bear in mind. People, however, did not rest satisfied with these limited analogies; but conceiving *music proper* to be a *kind of speech* (though more indefinite and subtle), they forthwith deduced its æsthetic laws from the properties of language. Every attribute and every effect of music was believed to have its analogy in speech. We ourselves are of opinion, that where the question turns on the specific nature of an art, the points in which it differs from cognate subjects are more important than its points of resemblance. An æsthetic enquiry, unswayed by such analogies which, though often tempting, do not affect the essence of music, must ever advance towards the point where speech and music irreconcilably part. Only from beyond this point may we hope to discover truly useful facts in respect of music. The fundamental difference consists in this : while *sound* in *speech* is but a sign, that is, a *means* for the purpose of expressing something which is quite distinct from its medium ; *sound* in *music* is the *end*, that is, the ultimate and absolute object in view. The intrinsic beauty of the musical forms in the latter case, and the exclusive dominion of thought over sound as a mere medium of expression, in the former, are so utterly distinct as to render the union of these two elements a logical impossibility.

Speech and music, therefore, have their centres of gravity at different points, around which the

characteristics of each are grouped ; and while all
specific *laws of music* will centre in its independent
forms of beauty, all *laws of speech* will turn upon the
correct use of sound as a medium of expressing
ideas.

The most baneful and confused notions have
sprung from the attempt to define music as a kind
of speech, and we may observe their practical consequences every day. Composers of feeble genius,
in particular, were only too ready to denounce as
false and sensual the ideal of intrinsic musical
beauty, because it was beyond their reach, and to
parade in its place the characteristic significance of
music. Quite irrespective of Richard Wagner's
operas, we often find in the most trivial instrumental
compositions disconnected cadences, recitatives, &c.,
which interrupt the flow of the melody, and which,
while startling the listener, affect to have some
*deep meaning*, though in reality they only display
want of beauty. Modern pieces, in which the
principal rhythm is constantly upset in order to
bring into prominence certain mysterious appendages
and a superabundance of glaring contrasts, are
praised for striving to pass the "narrow limits" of
music, and to elevate it to the rank of *speech*. Such
praise has always appeared to us somewhat am-
biguous. The limits of music are by no means
narrow, but they are clearly defined. Music can
never be "elevated to the rank of speech"—
musically speaking "lowered" would be a
more appropriate term—for music to be speech

at all would, of course, be a *superlative degree* of speech.*

Our singers always forget this, when in moments of intense emotion they ejaculate sentences as though they were *speaking*, and think they thus attain to the highest degree of musical expression. It does not strike them that the transition from song to speech is always a descent, so that the highest pitch of normal speech sounds deeper than the low notes in singing, though both proceed from the same

---

* We cannot conceal the fact that one of the loftiest productions of genius of all ages has by its grandeur contributed to this favourite fallacy of musical criticism of modern times, which assumes " an inherent propensity in music to become as definite as speech," and " to throw off the yoke of eurythmy." We allude to Beethoven's " *Ninth*." This Symphony is one of those intellectual watersheds which, visible from afar, and inaccessible, separate the currents of antagonistic beliefs.

Those musicians, who value above all things the sublimity of the " intention " and the intellectual importance of an aim distinct from the music, place the Ninth Symphony at the head of all music; while the small party who remain faithful to the abjured belief in intrinsic beauty and contend for purely æsthetic aspirations look upon it with qualified admiration. As may be guessed, it is the *Finale* which is the point at issue, since no difference of opinion is likely to arise among attentive and competent listeners respecting the exquisite, though not faultless beauty of the first three parts. We, ourselves, have always regarded the last part as nothing more than the gigantic shadow of a gigantic body. It is quite possible to realise and apprehend the mighty conception of a lonesome and despairing mind, reconciled at last by the thought of universal happiness, and yet to consider the music of the last part wanting in beauty, its genius and individuality notwithstanding. That this view of the Symphony is generally received with supreme disfavour we know but too well. In fact, when one of the most profound and accomplished of German scholars attacked the fundamental idea of the composition in the *Augsburger Allgem. Zeitung* in 1853, he at once felt the necessity of humorously describing the article as

organ. As mischievous in their practical consequences (if not more so, because of the impossibility of disproving them by actual experiment) are those *theories* which try to impose on music the laws of development and construction peculiar to speech, as in former days Rameau and Rousseau, and in modern times the disciples of Richard Wagner have endeavoured to do. In this attempt the life of the music is destroyed; the innate beauty of form annihilated in pursuit of the phantom " meaning."

---

emanating from a " feeble intellect." He demonstrated the æsthetic monstrosity of an instrumental composition of several parts closing with a *chorus*, and compared Beethoven to a sculptor, who carves the legs, the body, the chest, and the arms of a figure in white marble, but colours the head. One would think that all sensitive listeners must simultaneously experience a feeling of discomfort, when the sounds of the human voice suddenly break upon them, because at this point the composition " changes its centre of gravity with a " jerk and threatens to throw the listener off his balance." Nearly ten years later we had the satisfaction of knowing that the " feeble intellect " was none other than David Friedrich Strauss.

The clever Dr. Becher, on the other hand, who may figure as the representative of a whole class, speaks of the *fourth* part of the Ninth Symphony, in an essay printed in 1843, as a product of Beethoven's " genius which admits of no comparison with any existing com- " position in point of originality of construction, sublime organisation, " and boldness of imagination." He assures us that, in his opinion, this work, like Shakespeare's " ' King Lear,' and a dozen other " emanations of the human mind, in the zenith of poetic inspi- " ration, overtops even its peers—a very Dawalagiri in the Himalaya " of Art." Becher, in common with those who cherish the same views, gives an exhaustive *description* of the *significance* of the " subject " of each of the four parts and their profound symbolism—but about the *music itself* not a syllable is said. This is highly characteristic of a whole school of musical criticism, which to the question whether the *music* is beautiful, replies with a learned dissertation on its profound *meaning*.

G

One of the most important tasks of the æsthetics of
music would, therefore, be that of demonstrating
with inexorable logic the fundamental difference
between music and language, and of never departing
from the principle that, wherever the question is
a specifically musical one, all parallelisms with
language are wholly irrelevant.

# CHAPTER IV.

THOUGH, in our opinion, the chief and fundamental task of musical æsthetics consists in subordinating the supremacy, usurped by the feelings, to the legitimate one of beauty—since the organ of pure contemplation, from which, and for the sake of which, the truly beautiful flows, is not our emotional, but our imaginative faculty—yet the positive phenomena of the emotions play too striking and important a part in our musical life to admit of the question being settled by simply effecting this subordination.

However strictly an æsthetic analysis ought to be confined to the work of art itself, we should always remember that the latter constitutes the link between two living factors ; the *whence* and the *whither ;* in other words, between the composer and the listener, in whose minds the workings of the *imagination* are never so pure and unalloyed as the finished work itself represents them. ( Their imagination, on the contrary, is most intimately associated with feelings and sensations. The feelings, therefore, are of importance both *before* and *after* the completion of the work ; in respect of the composer first, and the listener afterwards, and this we dare not ignore.)

Let us consider the *composer.* During the act of composing he is in that exalted state of mind without which it seems impossible to raise the beautiful from the deep well of the imagination. That this exalted state of mind will, according to the composer's idiosyncrasy, take the form more or less of the nascent structure, now rising like billows and now subsiding into mere ripples, without ever becoming an emotional whirlpool which might wreck the powers of artistic invention; that calm reflection again is at least as essential as enthusiasm—all these are well-known principles of art. With special reference to the creative action of the *composer*, we should bear in mind that it always consists in the *grouping* and *fashioning* of musical elements. The sovereignty of the emotions, so falsely reputed to be the main factor in music, is nowhere more completely out of place than when it is supposed to govern the musician in the act of composing, and when the latter is regarded as a kind of inspired improvisation. The slowly progressing work of moulding a composition—which at the outset floated in mere outlines in the composer's brain—into a structure, clearly defined down to every bar; or possibly, without further preliminaries into the sensitive polymorphous form of orchestral music, requires quiet and subtle thought, such as none who have not actually essayed it can comprehend. Not only "fugato" or contrapuntal passages, but the most smoothly flowing Rondo and the most melodious air demand what our language so significantly calls an "elaboration" of the minutest details. The function of the composer is a *constructive* one within its own sphere, analogous to that of the sculptor. Like him, the composer must not allow his hands to be tied by anything alien to his material, since he, too, aims at giving an objective existence to his (musical) ideal, and at casting it into a pure form.

Rosenkranz may have overlooked this fact when he notices the paradox (without, however, explaining it) that *women*, who by nature are highly emotional beings, have achieved nothing as composers.[*] The cause, apart from the general reasons why women are less capable of mental achievements, is the plastic element in musical compositions which like sculpture and architecture, though in a different manner, imposes on us the necessity of keeping ourselves *free* from all subjective feelings. If the composing of music depended upon the intensity and vividness of our feelings, the complete want of female composers, as against the numerous authoresses and female painters, would be difficult to account for. It is not the feeling, but a specifically musical and technically-trained aptitude that enables us to compose. We think it, therefore, rather amusing to be gravely told by F. L. Schubart that the "masterly Andantes" of the composer Stanitz are the natural outcome of his tender heart;[†] or to be assured by Christian Rolle,[‡] that a loving and amiable disposition makes it possible for us to convert slow movements into masterpieces.

Nothing great or beautiful has ever been accomplished without warmth of feeling. The emotional faculty is, no doubt, highly developed in the

---

[*] Rosenkranz, " Psychologie," 2nd edition, page 60.

[†] Schubart, " Ideen zu einer Æsthetik der Tonkunst," 1806.

[‡] " Neue Wahrnehmungen zur Aufnahme der Musik." Berlin, 1784. Page 102.

composer, no less than in the poet; but with the former
it is not the productive factor. A strong and definite
pathos may fill his soul and be the consecrating
impulse to many a work, but it can never become
the subject-matter, as is obvious from the very
nature of music which has neither the power nor
the vocation to represent definite feelings.

An *inward melody*, so to speak, and not mere
feeling prompts the true musician to compose.

We have tried to show that the composing of
music is *constructive* in its nature and, as such, it is
purely *objective*. The composer creates something
intrinsically beautiful, while the inexhaustible
intellectual associations of sound enable his subjectivity to reflect itself in the mode of the formative
process. Every musical note having its individual
complexion, the prominent characteristics of the
composer, such as sentimentality, energy, cheerfulness, &c., may through the preference given by him
to certain keys, rhythms, and modulations be traced
in those *general* phenomena which music is capable
of reproducing. But once they become part and
parcel of the composition, they interest us only as
musical features; as the character of the composition,
not of the composer.* That which a sentimental,

---

* How careful we ought to be when inferring from a composition
the character of its composer, and how great the risk is that flights
of fancy will take the place of dispassionate research at the expense of
truth, has among other instances been shown by the Beethoven
biography of A. B. Marx, who based his panegyric on musical pre-
dilections, and scorning a conscientious investigation of facts, had
many of his conclusions categorically refuted by Thayer's exhaustive
enquiry.

an ingenious, a graceful, or a sublime composer produces, is, above all, *music*, an objective image. Their works will differ from one another by unmistakable characteristics, and each in its complete form will reflect the author's individuality ; but all, without exception, were created as independent and purely musical forms of beauty.

It is not the actual feeling of the composer, not a subjective state of mind, that evokes a like feeling in the listener. By conceding to music the power to evoke feelings, we tacitly recognise the cause to be something objective in the music, since it is only the objective element in beauty which can possess the quality of *irresistibleness*. This objective something is, in this case, the purely *musical* features of a composition. It is, æsthetically, quite correct to speak of a theme as having a sad or noble accent, but not as expressing the sad or noble feelings of the composer. Even more irrelevant to the character of a composition are the social or political events of the period. The *musical* expression of the theme necessarily follows from the individual selection of the musical factors. That this selection is due to psychological causes or facts of contemporary history has to be proved by the particular work itself (and not simply by dates or the composer's birthplace), and even when thus established, the connection, however interesting it may be, remains a fact belonging solely to history or biography. An *æsthetic* analysis can take no note of circumstances which lie outside the work itself.

Though it is certain that the individuality

of the composer will find a symbolic expression in his works, it would be a gross error from this subjective aspect of the question to deduce conceptions, the true explanation of which is to be found in the objectiveness of the artistic creation. One of these conceptions is *style*.*

Style in music, we should like to be understood in a purely *musical* sense: as the perfect grasp of the technical side of music, which in the expression of the creative thought assumes an appearance of uniformity. A composer shows his "good style" by avoiding everything trivial, futile and unsuitable, as he carries out a clearly conceived idea, and by bringing every technical detail into artistic agreement with the whole. With Vischer ("Æsthetik," § 527) we would use the word "style" in music also in an absolute sense, and disregarding the historical and individual meanings of the term, apply the word "style" to a composer, as we apply the word "character" to a man.

The *architectonic* side of beauty in music is brought into bold relief by the question of style. The laws of *style* being of a more subtle nature than the laws of mere proportion, one single bar if out of keeping with the rest, though perfect in itself, will vitiate the style. Just as in architecture we might call a

---

* Forkel is, therefore, quite mistaken in his derivation of the various musical styles, from " different modes of thought." According to him "the style of a composer is due to the romantic, the " conceited, the apathetic, the puerile, or the pedantic carrying " bombast, arrogance, coldness, and affectation into the expression of " his thoughts." (" Theorie der Musik," 1777, page 23.)

certain arabesque out of place, so we should condemn as bad style a cadence or modulation which is opposed to the unity of the fundamental thought. The term unity must, of course, be understood in its wider and loftier acceptation, since it may comprise contrast, episode, and other such departures.

The limits to which a musical composition can bear the impress of the author's own personal temperament are fixed by a pre-eminently objective and plastic process.

The act in which the direct outflow of a feeling into sound may take place is not so much the *invention* of music as its *reproduction*. The fact that from a philosophical point of view a composition is the *finished* work of art, irrespective of its performance, should not prevent us from paying attention to the division of music into composition and reproduction (one of the most significant classifications of our art) whenever it contributes to the explanation of some phenomenon.

Its value is especially manifest on enquiring into the subjective impression which music produces. The *player* has the privilege of venting directly through his instrument the feeling by which he is swayed at the time, and to breathe into his performance passionate excitement, ardent longing, buoyant strength, and joy. The mere physical impulse which directly communicates the inward tremor as the fingers touch the strings, as the hand draws the bow, or as the vocal chords vibrate in song, enables the executant to pour forth his inmost feelings. His subjectiveness thus makes itself

directly heard in the *music* and is not merely a silent
prompter.  The work of the composer is slow and
intermittent, whereas that of the player is an unimpeded flight; the former composes for time, the
latter performs for the fruition of the moment.  The
piece of music is worked out by the composer, but it
is the performance which we enjoy.  Thus the
active and emotional principle in music occurs in the
act of reproduction, which draws the electric spark
from a mysterious source and directs it towards the
heart of the listener.  The player can, of course,
give only what the composition contains, and little
more than a correct rendering of the notes is
demanded of him; he has merely to divine and
expose the spirit of the *composer*—true, but it is the
spirit of the *player* which is revealed in this act of
reproduction.  The same piece wearies or charms
us, according to the life infused into its performance.
It is like one and the same person whom we picture
to ourselves, now in a state of rapturous enthusiasm,
and now in his apathetic every-day looks.  Though
the most ingenious musical box fails to move us, a
simple itinerant musician, who puts his whole soul
into a song, may do so.

A state of mind manifests itself most directly in
music when origination and execution coincide.
This occurs in the freest form of *extempore playing*,
and if the player proceeds not so much according to
the strict methods of art as with a predominantly
subjective tendency (a pathological one, in a wider
sense), the expression which he elicits from the keys
may assume almost the vividness of speech.  Who-

ever has enjoyed this absolute freedom of speech, in total oblivion of all surroundings, this spontaneous revelation of his inner self, will know without further explanation how love, jealousy, joy, and sorrow rush out of their secret recesses, undisguised and yet secure, celebrating their own triumphs, singing their own lays, and fighting their own battles, until their lord and master calls them back, quieted, and yet disquieting.

While the player gives vent to his emotions the expression of that which is played is imparted to the *listener*. Let us now turn to the latter.

We often see him deeply impressed by a piece, moved with joy or grief; his whole being rising far above purely æsthetic enjoyment; now enraptured and now profoundly depressed. The existence of such effects is undeniable, actual, and genuine, attaining at times supreme degrees, and they are, moreover, so notorious that we need not dwell any further on their description. Here only two questions arise: in what respect the specific character of this excitation of the feelings by *music* differs from other emotions, and to what extent this operation is *æsthetic*.

Though *all* arts, without exception, have the power to act on our feelings, yet the mode in which *music* displays it is, undoubtedly, peculiar to this art *alone*. Music operates on our emotional faculty with greater intenseness and rapidity than the product of any other art. A few chords may give rise to a frame of mind which a poem can induce only by a lengthy exposition, or a picture by

prolonged contemplation, despite the fact that the arts
to which the latter belong boast the advantage over
music of having at their service the whole range of
ideas on which we know our feelings of joy or sorrow
to depend. The action of sound is not only more
sudden, but also more powerful and direct. The
other arts persuade us, but music takes us by surprise. This, its characteristic sway over our
feelings, is most vividly realised when we are in a
state of unusual exaltation or depression.

In states of mind where paintings and poetry,
statues, and architectural beauties fail to rouse us to
active interest, *music* will still have power over us—
nay, greater power than at other times. Whoever
is obliged to hear or play music while in a state of
painful excitement, will feel it like vinegar sprinkled
on a wound. No other art, under equal conditions,
can cut so sharply to the very quick. The form and
character of the music lose their distinctiveness; be
it a gloomy Adagio or a sparkling Waltz, we are
unable to tear ourselves away from the sounds—we
are not conscious of the composition as such, but
only of sound, of music, as an undefined and demo-
niacal power, sending a thrill through every nerve of
our body.

When Goethe in his old age experienced once
again the power of love, a sensibility for music
arose, such as he had never dreamt of before.
Referring to those remarkable days at Marienbad
(1823) in a letter to Zelter, he says: "What a
" stupendous power music now has over me! Milder's
" voice, Szymanowska's richness of tone,—nay, the

" very performances of the Yagercorps band open my
" heart like a clenched fist opens to greet a friend.
" I am firmly convinced that during the first bar I
" should have to leave your singing academy." Too
clear-sighted not to ascribe the effect mainly to
*nervous* excitement, Goethe concludes in the
following terms : " You would cure me of a kind of
" morbid excitability, which is, after all, at the bottom
" of this phenomenon."* From this alone it ought to
be clear that the musical excitation of our feelings
is often due to other than purely æsthetic factors.
A purely æsthetic factor appeals to our nervous
system in its normal condition, and does not
count on a morbid exaltation or depression of the
mind.

The fact of its operating with greater intensity on
our nerves proves music to have a preponderance
of power as compared with other arts. But on
closely examining this preponderance, we find it to
be *qualitative,* and its distinctive quality to depend
upon *physiological* conditions. The material element,
which in all æsthetic enjoyment is at the root of the
intellectual one, is greater in music than in any
other art. Music, through its immateriality the
most ethereal art, and yet the most sensuous one
through its play of forms without any extraneous
subject, exhibits in this mysterious fusion of two
antagonistic principles a strong affinity for the
*nerves,* these equally mysterious links in the invisible
telegraphic connection between mind and body.

---

* „ Briefwechsel zwischen Goethe und Zelter," Vol. III., page 332.

Psychologists and physiologists alike are fully cognizant of the truth that music acts most powerfully *on the nervous system*, but neither of them, unfortunately, can offer an adequate explanation. *Psychologists* will never be able to throw any light on the irresistible force with which certain chords, " timbres," and melodies impress the entire human organism, the difficulty being to establish a nexus between certain nerve excitations and certain states of mind. Nor has the marvellously successful science of *physiology* made any vital discovery towards a solution of this problem.

As regards the musical monographies of this hybrid subject, they nearly all invest music with the imposing halo of a miracle-worker and descant on some brilliant examples, rather than institute a scientific enquiry into the true and necessary relation between music and our consciousness. Of such an enquiry alone are we in need, and not of the blind faith of a doctor Albrecht, who prescribes music as a diaphoretic, nor of the incredulity of an Oerstedt, who explains the howling of a dog on hearing music in certain keys, by supposing the dog to have been specially trained to it by a system of whipping.*

Many lovers of music may not be aware that there is quite a literature on the physiological action of music and its therapeutic application. Rich in interesting curiosities, but alike unreliable in their observations and unscientific in their explanations,

---

* " Der Geist der Natur," III., 9.

most of these musical quacks magnify a highly composite and secondary endowment of music into one of unconditional efficiency.

From the time of Pythagoras (the first, it is said, to effect miraculous cures by means of music) down to the present day, the doctrine has appeared again and again (enriched, however, by fresh examples rather than by new discoveries), that the exciting or soothing effect of music on the human organism may be utilised as a remedy for numerous diseases. Peter Lichtenthal gives us a detailed account ("Der musikalische Arzt") of the cure of *gout, sciatica, epilepsy, the plague, catalepsy, delirium, convulsions, typhus,* and even *stupidity (stupiditas)* merely by the power of music.*

These writers may be divided into two classes according to their *method of proof*.

One class, arguing from the *material* point of view, seek to establish the curative effect of music by the physical action of the sound-waves which, say they, are transmitted by the auditory nerve to the whole nervous system, and the general shock thus resulting induces a salutary reaction in the morbid part of the organism. The feelings arising at the same time are, it is contended, merely the effect of the

---

* This doctrine reached the height of confusion with the celebrated doctor Battista Porta, who, combining the ideas of a medicinal plant and a musical instrument, professed to cure dropsy by means of a flute made from the stalk of the hellebore. A musical instrument, made from the wood of the poplar (Populus) was to cure sciatica, and one made of cinnamon bark was to cure fainting fits. (*Encyclopédie*, article " Musique.")

nervous shock, since not only do emotions produce bodily changes, but the latter, in their turn, may produce corresponding emotions.

According to this theory (championed by an Englishman named Webb), which counts among its followers men like Nicolai, Schneider, Lichtenthal, J. J. Engel, Sulzer, and others, music operates on us just as the peals of an organ do on doors and windows, which tremble under the aerial vibrations. In support of this theory cases are mentioned such as that of Boyle's servant, whose gums commenced to bleed on hearing a saw sharpened, or of people falling into convulsions when the edge of a knife is scraped on glass.

But that is not music, properly so called. The fact that music, in common with those phenomena which so strongly affect our nerves, has sound for its substratum will be found to be one of great importance in respect of certain conclusions to be drawn hereafter; but for our present purpose it is enough to emphasize the truth, in opposition to a materialistic view, that music begins where those isolated auditory impressions terminate, and that the feeling of sadness which an Adagio may awake, and the bodily sensation produced by a shrill or discordant sound, are totally different in kind.

The other class of writers (to which belong Kausch and most writers on æsthetics) try to explain the therapeutic effect of music on *psychological* grounds. Music, they argue, arouses emotions and passions which throw the nervous system into a violent agitation, and a violent agitation of the nervous system produces a healthy reaction in the diseased organism. This train of reasoning, the logical defects of which are too obvious to require specification, is carried so far by these idealistic " psychologists," in defiance of the materialistic school of thought and in utter disregard of the truths of physiology, as to deny, on the authority of an Englishman of the name of Whytt, the connection between the auditory nerve and the other nerves, which, of course, involves the impossibility of *bodily* transmitting to the entire organism an impressio produced on the ear.

The notion of awakening by musical means definite feelings such as love, sadness, anger, and delight, which in their turn are to cure the body by salutary excitement, is certainly a plausible one. It always reminds us of the amusing verdict of one of our most distinguished scientists respecting "Goldberg's electro-magnetic chains." It was not proved, he said, whether an electric current was capable of curing certain diseases, but it was proved beyond doubt that " Goldberg's chains " were incapable of generating an electric current. Applied to our " musical doctors," this would run thus : It is *possible* that certain emotions may bring about a favourable turn in bodily ailments, but it is *impossible* to call forth at will definite emotions by musical means.

Both theories—the psychological and the physiological—agree in this, that they infer from questionable premises even more questionable conclusions, and that their *practical* application is the most

questionable of all. It may be quite admissible to
justify some method of treatment on logical grounds,
but it is rather disagreeable that there is no record
of a doctor sending his patient to hear Meyerbeer's
" Prophet " in order to cure him of typhus,
or of the French horn being used instead of the
lancet.

The physical action of music is neither so powerful in itself, nor so certain, nor yet so independent
of psychological and æsthetic associations, nor can
it be so nicely regulated, as to admit of its being
seriously considered as a remedy.

Every cure effected by the aid of music must be
regarded in the light of an exception, and the success
can never be put down to the music alone, being due
partly to special causes and often merely to the
patient's idiosyncrasy. It is highly significant that
the only case in which music is really applied as a
remedy is in the treatment of the insane, and this is
mainly grounded on the psychological aspect of
musical impressions. That in the modern treatment
of insanity music is frequently employed with great
success is a well-known fact. The success, however,
is owing neither to the nervous shock nor to the
arousing of the passions, but to the soothing and
exhilarating influence which music, at once diverting
and fascinating, exerts on a darkened or morbidly
excited mind. It is true that the patient listens to
the sensuous, rather than to the artistic part of
the music—yet, if he can but fix his attention, he
proves himself capable of æsthetic enjoyment, though
in an inferior degree.

Now, in what respect do all these musico-medical works contribute towards a clear knowledge of music ? They all confirm what has been observed from time immemorial—namely, (that with the "feelings" and "passions" aroused by music there always co-exists a strong physical agitation) Once grant the assumption that an integrant part of the emotion aroused by music is of *physical* origin, and it follows that the phenomenon, closely related as it is to nerve function, must be studied in this, its physical aspect. No musician, therefore, can expect a scientific solution of this problem without making himself acquainted with the latest results of *physiological* research into the connection between music and the emotions.

If we follow the course which a melody must take in order to operate on our feelings, we shall find it traced with tolerable accuracy from the vibrating instrument to the auditory nerve, thanks especially to Helmholtz's famous discoveries in this domain of science recorded in his work, " Lehre von den Tonempfindungen." The science of acoustics has clearly shown what the outward conditions are, under which the sensation of sound in general, and of any sound in particular, becomes possible ; anatomy, by the help of the microscope, has revealed the most minute and secret structures of the organ of hearing ; physiology, in fine, though debarred from experimenting directly on the extremely small and delicate constituents of this hidden marvel has, nevertheless, to a certain extent, ascertained its *modus operandi*, and to a still greater

extent explained it by a theory propounded by
Helmholtz, so as to render the whole process
by which we become conscious of sound physiologically intelligible. Even beyond these limits,
in the domain where natural science comes into
close contact with æsthetics, much has been
elucidated by Helmholtz's theory of consonance
and the affinities of sound, which until lately was
shrouded in mystery. But this, unfortunately, is the
whole extent of our knowledge. The most essential
part, the physiological process by which the
*sensation* of sound is converted into a *feeling*, a *state
of mind*, is unexplained, and will ever remain so.
Physiologists know that what our senses perceive as
sound is, objectively speaking, molecular motion
within the nerve substance, and this is true of the
nerve-centres no less than of the auditory nerve.
They also know that the fibres of the auditory nerve
are connected with the other nerves, to which they
transmit the impulse received, and that the organ of
hearing is connected with the cerebrum and the
cerebellum, with the larynx, the lungs, and the heart.
About the specific mode, however, in which music
affects these nerves they know nothing, nor yet
about the different ways in which certain musical
factors, such as chords, rhythms, and the sounds of
instruments operate on different nerves. Is a
sensation of musical sound propagated to all the
nerves connected with the auditory nerve, or only to
some of them ? With what degree of intensity?
Which musical elements affect the brain more
particularly, and which the nerves supplying the

heart and the lungs ? It is an undoubted fact that dance-music produces in young people, whose natural inclination is not controlled by social restraints, a twitching of the whole body, and especially of the feet. We cannot, without being one-sided, dispute the *physiological* action of martial or dance music, and attribute its effect solely to a *psychological* association of ideas. Its psychological aspect—the recollection of former pleasures derived from dancing—helps us to understand the phenomenon ; but taken alone it does not explain it. The feet do not move because it is dance-music, but we call it dance-music because it makes the feet move. Whoever glances around in an opera house will notice ladies involuntarily beating the time with their heads to any lively or taking tune, but never to an Adagio, however impressive and melodious it may be. Should we infer from this that certain musical factors, and more particularly rhythmical ones, affect the motor and others the sensory nerves ? Which affect the former and which the latter ?* Is the solar plexus, which is reputed to

---

\* Carus tries to account for the motory stimulus by supposing the auditory nerve to originate in the cerebellum ; the latter to be the seat of volition ; and the co-operation of the two to be the cause of the phenomenon, that auditory impressions incite us to acts of courage, &c. But this is a very lame hypothesis, seeing that science has not yet proved the auditory nerve to originate in the cerebellum. Harless (see R. Wagner's Manual of Physiology, " The function of hearing ") maintains that the mere *perception of rhythmical motion*, apart from auditory impressions, has the same tendency to give motory impulses as rhythmical music. But this doctrine conflicts with our experience.

be pre-eminently the seat of sensation, especially affected by music? Or is it the sympathetic ganglia (the best part of which is their name, as Purkinje once remarked to me) which are so affected? Why one sound affects us as shrill and harsh, another one as clear and mellifluous, the science of acoustics explains by the irregularity or regularity with which the sonorous pulses follow each other; again, that several simultaneously occurring sounds produce now the effect of consonance, and now that of dissonance, is accounted for by the slow or rapid succession of beats.* The explanations of more or less simple *sensations of sound*, however, cannot satisfy the æsthetic enquirer, who demands an explanation of the *feeling* produced, and asks—how it is that one series of melodious sounds induces a feeling of sadness, and another, of equally melodious sounds, a feeling of joy? Whence the diametrically opposed moods which often take hold of us with irresistible force on hearing chords and instruments of different kinds, but of equally pure and agreeable sound?

To all this—at least as far as our knowledge and judgment go—physiologists can give no clue! How, indeed, can they be expected to do so? For they can tell us neither why grief makes us weep, nor why joy makes us laugh—nay, they do not even know what grief and joy are! Let us, therefore, never appeal

---

* Helmholtz, "Lehre von den Tonempfindungen," 2nd edition, 1870, page 319.

to a science for explanations which it cannot possibly give.*

It is true, of course, that the cause of every emotion which music arouses is chiefly to be found in some specific mode of nerve activity induced by an auditory impression. But how the excitation of the auditory nerve (which we cannot even trace to its source) is transformed into a definite sentiment; how a physical impression can pass into a state of mind; how, in fine, a sensation can become an emotion—all this lies beyond the mysterious bridge which no philosopher has ever crossed. It is the one great problem expressed in numberless ways : the connection between mind and body. This Sphinx will never throw herself into the sea.†

All that the enquiries into the physiological aspect of music have brought to light is of the utmost importance for the correct appreciation of auditory impressions as such, and in that direction

---

* Lotze, one of our most gifted physiologists, says ("Medicinische Psychologie," p. 237): "A careful study of *melodies* would extort from "us the admission that *we know nothing whatever about the conditions* "under which the change from one kind of nerve excitation to another "becomes the physical substratum of the powerful æsthetic feelings "which vary with the music." With respect to the feeling of satisfaction or discomfort which a single tone may evoke, he remarks (p. 236): "It is a matter of utter impossibility to offer a physiological "explanation for these simple sensations. in particular, as we do not "know with any degree of accuracy in what respect the impressing "causes affect the nerve function, and we are, therefore, quite unable "to determine to what extent they promote or impede it."

† While revising the fourth edition of this work, the author came across a most invaluable corroboration of the views here set forth, in Dubois-Reymonds' Speech in the Science Congress of 1872, in Leipzig.

considerable progress may yet be made. But with respect to the main issue in music, we shall probably never know more than we do now.

The result thus arrived at, when applied to musical æsthetics, leads to the conclusion that those theorists who ground the beautiful in music on the feelings it excites build upon a most uncertain foundation, scientifically speaking, since they are necessarily quite ignorant of the nature of this connection, and can therefore, at best, only indulge in speculations and flights of fancy. An interpretation of music based on the feelings cannot be acceptable either to art or science. A critic does not substantiate the merit or subject of a symphony by describing his subjective feelings on hearing it, nor can he enlighten the student by making the feelings the starting-point of his argument. This is of great moment; for if the connection between certain feelings and certain modes of musical expression were so well established as some seem inclined to think, and as it ought to be if the importance claimed for it were justified, it would be an easy matter to lead the young composer onwards to the most sublime heights of his art. The attempt to do this has actually been made. Mattheson teaches in the third chapter of his " Vollkommener Capellmeister," how pride, humility, and all the other emotions and passions are to be translated into music. Thus he says : " To express jealousy, the " music must have something grim, sullen, and " doleful about it." Heinchen, another writer of the last century, devotes eight pages in his " Generalbass " to actual examples of the modes in which music should express the "feelings of an impetuous, "factious, pompous, timorous, or love-sick mind."* To crown the absurdity, directions of this kind should commence with the formula of cookery-books: " Take," &c., or with that of medical prescriptions, " R." Such attempts yield the highly instructive lesson that specific rules of art are always both too narrow and too wide.

These inherently fallacious precepts for the excitation of definite emotions by musical means have so much the less to do with æsthetics, as the effect aimed at is not a purely æsthetic one, an inseparable portion of it being of a distinctly *physical* character. An *æsthetic* prescription would have to teach the composer how to produce beauty in music, and not how to excite particular feelings in the audience. How impotent these rules are in reality is best proved by considering what magic power they must possess to be efficacious. (For if the action of every musical factor on our feelings were a necessary and determinable one, we should be able to play on the mind of the listener, as on the keyboard of a piano. And even assuming this to be possible—would the object of music be attained thereby?) This is the only

---

* Greatly amusing are the discourses of v. Böcklin, Privy Councillor and Doctor of Philosophy, who (on page 34) in his book, " Fragmente zur höheren Musik " (1811), says among other things: " If the composer wants to represent an offended person, outbursts " of æsthetic warmth must follow each other in rapid succession ; lofty " strains must resound with extreme vivacity ; the barytones rave, and " terrific blasts inspire the expectant listener with awe."

legitimate form of the question, and to it none but a negative reply can be given.  *Musical beauty* alone is the true power which the composer wields.  With this for his pilot, he safely passes through the rapids of time, where the factor of emotion would be powerless to save him from shipwreck.

The two points at issue—namely, what the distinctive trait is of a feeling aroused by music, and whether this is of an essentially æsthetic nature— are settled by the recognition of one and the same fact : the intense action on our *nervous system*.  This fact explains the characteristic force and directness with which music (as compared with arts that do not employ the medium of *sound*) is capable of exciting emotions.

But the more overpowering the effect is in a physical—*i.e.*, in a pathological sense, the less is it due to *æsthetic* causes ; a proposition, by the way, the terms of which cannot be inverted.  In connection with the production and interpretation of music, another factor must be emphasized, which in antithesis to a specifically musical excitation of the feelings, approximates to the general æsthetic conditions of all the other arts.  This factor is the act of *pure contemplation* (die reine Anschauung).  The next chapter will be devoted to the study of its specific function in music, and of the manifold relations subsisting between it and our sensibility.

## CHAPTER V.

THE greatest obstacle to a scientific development of musical æsthetics has been the undue prominence given to the action of music on our feelings. The more violent this action is, the louder is it praised as evidence of musical beauty. But we have seen that the most powerful effects of music are mainly to be attributed to *physical* excitement on the part of the listener. The power which music possesses of profoundly affecting the nervous system cannot be ascribed so much to the *artistic* forms created by, and appealing to the mind, as to the *material* with which music works and which Nature has endowed with certain inscrutable affinities of a physiological order. That which for the unguarded feelings of so many lovers of music forges the fetters which they are so fond of clanking, are the *primitive elements* of music—*sound* and *motion*. Far be it from us to loosen the legitimate ties which connect music with the emotions, but the latter, which more or less always co-exist with the act of pure contemplation, are of æsthetic value only so long as we remain conscious of their æsthetic origin ; that is, so long as the pleasure is solely derived from viewing *a thing of beauty*, and *a thing of beauty* just in this particular form.

Where this consciousness is absent ; where, while contemplating the work of art, we are labouring under other influences ; where the mind is carried away by the purely physical element of sound, *art*, in the true sense of the word, can pride itself the less on having produced this effect the stronger the effect is. The number of those who thus listen to, or rather feel music, is very considerable. While in a state of passive receptivity they suffer only what is elemental in music to affect them, and thus pass into a vague " supersensible " excitement of the senses, produced by the general drift of the composition. Their attitude towards music is not an observant but a *pathological* one. They are, as it were, in a state of waking dreaminess and lost in a sounding nullity, their mind is constantly on the rack of suspense and expectancy. If to a musician who considers the supreme aim of music to be the excitation of feelings we present several pieces, say of a gay and sprightly character, they will all impress him alike. His feelings assimilate only what these pieces have in common, but the special features of the composition and the individuality of its artistic interpretation pass unnoticed. The truly musical listener, however, pursues an exactly opposite course. His attention is so greatly absorbed by the particular form and character of the composition, by that which gives it the stamp of individuality among a dozen pieces of similar complexion, that he pays but little heed to the question whether the expression of the same or of different feelings is aimed at. The habit of looking only for some abstract feeling, instead of judging the concrete work of art is, in any great measure, practised in music alone. It may be likened to the peculiar effect of *light* on a landscape, which strikes some people so forcibly as to prevent them from clearly perceiving the illuminated object itself. A general impression, unreasoned and therefore doubly obtrusive, thrusts itself upon their indiscriminating senses.*

Instead of closely following the course of the music, these enthusiasts, reclining in their seats and only half-awake, suffer themselves to be rocked and lulled by the mere flow of sound. The sound now waxing and now diminishing in strength ; now rising up in jubilant strains and now softly dying away, produces in them a series of vague sensations which they in their simplicity fancy to be the result of intellectual action. They are the most easily satisfied part of the audience, and it is also they who tend to lower the dignity of music. For their ear the æsthetic criterion of *intelligent* gratification is wanting, and a good cigar, some exquisite dainty, or a warm bath yields them the same enjoyment as a Symphony,

---

*The love-sick *Duke* in Shakespeare's " Twelfth Night " is a poetic personification of this mode of hearing music. He says :

> " If music be the food of love, play on,
>   Give me excess of it," &c.

> " Oh, it came o'er my ear like the sweet South
>   That breathes upon a bank of violets
>   Stealing and giving odour."

and later on, in the second Act, he exclaims :

> " Give me some music," &c.,
> " Methought it did relieve my passion much," &c.

though they may not be aware of the fact.  In the indolent and apathetic attitude of some and the hysterical raptures of others, the active principle is the same—delight in the *elemental* property of music. To recent times, by the way, we owe a discovery of the greatest moment for such listeners as merely wish their feelings to be played upon to the exclusion of their intellect, the discovery of a far more potent factor than music.  We are alluding to ether and chloroform.  There is no doubt that these anæsthetics envelop the whole organism in a cloud of delightful and dreamlike sensations, so that there is no longer any need for stooping to the vulgar practice of wine-bibbing, though it must be confessed that this, too, is not without its musical effect.

From this point of view, musical compositions belong to the class of *spontaneous products of nature*, the contemplation of which charms us, without obliging us to enter into the thoughts of a creative mind, conscious of what it creates.  The sweet exhalations of the acacia may be breathed with closed eyes and in a dream, as it were; but creations of the human intellect demand a different attitude of mind, unless we would drag them down to the level of mere physical stimulants.

No other art lends itself so readily to such practices as music, the physical side of which admits the possibility at least of an unreasoning enjoyment. The *fugitive nature* of sound, as compared with the *enduring* effect of other arts, reminds us most significantly of the act of imbibing.

We may drink in a melody, but not a picture, a church, or a drama. For this reason no other art can be turned to such subservient uses. Even the best music may be performed at a *banquet*, and promote the assimilation of indigestible food. Music is at once the most imperative and the most indulgent of all arts. A barrel-organ at our door may force us to *hear* it, but not even a Symphony by Mendelssohn can compel us to *listen*.

This objectionable mode of hearing music is by no means identical with the naïve delight which the uncultured masses take in the material aspect of the various arts, while its ideal aspect is manifest only to the trained understanding of the few. The unartistic interpretation of a piece of music is derived, on the contrary, not from the material part properly so-called, not from the rich variety of the successions of sounds, but from their vague aggregate effect, which impresses them as an undefinable feeling. This explains the unique position which the *intellectual element* in music occupies in relation to *form* and *substance* (subject). The sentiment pervading a piece of music is habitually regarded as the drift, the idea, the spirit of the composition; whereas the artistic and original combination of definite successions of sound is said to be the mere form, the mould, the material garb of those supersensible elements. But it is precisely the " specifically-musical " element of the creation of inventive genius which the contemplating mind apprehends and assimilates. These concrete musical images, and not the vague impression of some abstract feeling, constitute the spirit of the composition. The *form* (the musical structure) is the real *substance* (subject) of music—in fact, is the music itself, in antithesis to the feeling, its alleged subject, which can be called neither its subject nor its form, but simply the effect produced. In like manner that which is regarded as purely *material*, as the transmitting medium, is the product of a thinking mind, whereas that which is presumed to be the subject—the emotional effect—belongs to the *physical* properties of sound, the greater part of which is governed by *physiological* laws.

The above considerations enable us to put down at its true value the so-called *" moral effect"* of music, which is paraded before us as a brilliant counterpart to the already mentioned *"physical effect,"* and which was expatiated on so often by older writers. But music in this sense is not in the remotest degree enjoyed as a thing of beauty, since it acts like a brute force of Nature and may incite us to the most senseless actions. Its function, therefore, is diametrically opposed to truly æsthetic enjoyment, and it is obvious that the alleged moral and the acknowledged physical effects of music have a good deal in common.

The importunate creditor, who by his debtor's music is induced to forgive him the whole debt,* is affected in the same manner as one who by the tune of a waltz is suddenly roused from repose and

---

* This is related of the Neapolitan singer Palma, and of others.
(" Anecdotes on Music," by A. Burgh, 1814.)

impelled to dance.   The former is moved by the
subtle elements of harmony and melody, the latter
by the more palpable one of rhythm.   Neither of
them acts of his own free will, neither of them is
overwhelmed by a superior mind or by moral beauty,
but simply in consequence of a powerful nervous
stimulus.   Music loosens the feet or the heart just
as wine loosens the tongue.   But such victories only
testify to the weakness of the vanquished.   To be
the slave of unreasoning, undirected, and purposeless
feelings, ignited by a power which is out of all
relation to our will and intellect, is not worthy of the
human mind.   If people allow themselves to be so
completely carried away by what is elemental in
art as to lose all self-control, this scarcely redounds
to the glory of the art, and much less to that of the
individual.

It is by no means the object of music to handicap
the mind with such tendencies, but its intense
action on the emotional faculty renders an enjoyment
in this sense, at all events, possible.   This is the
cause of the oldest attacks on music, grounded on
the reproach that it enervates, effeminates, and
benumbs its votaries.

And this reproach is but too well merited wherever
music is performed only to excite "indefinite feelings"
and to supply food for the "emotions."   Beethoven
wanted music "to strike fire in the mind," at least
"it ought to do so," he thought.   But is it not just
possible that the fire kindled and fed by *music* may
prevent the development of that strength of will and
power of intellect which man is capable of?

I

This stricture on the influence of music seems to us, in any case, more dignified than extravagant praises. As the *physical* effect of music varies with the morbid excitability of the nervous system, so the *moral* influence of sound is in proportion to the crudeness of mind and character. The lower the degree of culture, the greater the potency of the agent in question. It is well known that the action of music is most powerful of all in the case of savages.

But that does not discourage these experts in musical ethics. They love to quote as a kind of introduction the numerous instances of " animals even " yielding to the power of music. It is true that the sound of the trumpet inspires, the horse with courage and an eagerness for the battle, that the fiddle tempts the bear to waltz, and that both the nimble spider and the clumsy elephant move to its fascinating strains. But is it, after all, so great an honour to be a musical enthusiast in *such* company ?

After these animal accomplishments come the attainments of man. They are mostly of the kind related of Alexander the Great, who became furious on hearing Timotheus perform on the flute, and cooled down under the influence of a song. The less notorious Ericus Bonus, King of Denmark, in order to convince himself of the famous power of music, summoned a renowned musician to play before him, but not until every kind of weapon was put out of reach. By the choice of his modulations, the minstrel first cast on all around him a gloom,

which he presently changed into hilarity. This
hilarity he gradually worked up into a feeling of
frenzy. " Even the king rushed out of the room,
" seized his sword, and slew four of the bystanders."
(Albert Krantzius ; dan. lib. v., cap. 3.) And that,
be it noted, was " Eric the good."

If such " moral effects " of music were still in
vogue, we should probably be in too chronic a state
of indignation ever to have the mental calm necessary for a dispassionate survey of this weird power,
which with arrogant " exterritorialness " subjugates
and confuses the human mind, without in the least
regarding its thoughts and resolutions.

The reflection, however, that the most famous of
these musical trophies have been won in the
remote past, inclines us to view them in the light
of history only.

It is beyond all question that the action of music
was far more direct in the case of ancient races
than it is with us, because mankind is much more
easily impressed by *elemental forces* in a primitive
state of culture than later on, when intellectual
consciousness and the faculty of reflection have
attained a higher degree of maturity. This natural
sensitiveness was greatly assisted by the peculiar
condition of music during the Grecian era. Music
of that era was no *art* in the present acceptation of
the term. *Sound* and *rhythm* discharged their
functions in almost isolated independence, and in their
poverty-stricken ostentation took the place of those
rich and ingenious forms which constitute the music of
our days. All we know about the music of those

times points to the conclusion that its function was purely sensuous, though, within such limits, susceptible of considerable refinement. Judged by the modern standard of art, there was no such thing as music in the age of the ancient classics; otherwise it would never have disappeared, but would have played just as important a part in the subsequent development of the art, as classical poetry, sculpture, and architecture have done. The love of the Greeks for a profound study of their extremely subtle relations of sound is a purely scientific question and foreign to the present enquiry.

The lack of harmony, the poverty of the melody within the extremely narrow limits of the Recitative, and finally the impossibility of expanding the ancient system into a multiformity of truly musical images absolutely disqualified music, as then understood, for the position of an art in a musical sense. Nor had it any really independent function, being always used in connection with poetry, dancing, and pantomimic representation; in other words, as an adjunct of other arts. The sole office of music was to give life to the rhythmical beats, to the sounds of the various instruments, and lastly, as an intensification of *declamatory recitative*, to comment words and feelings. The action of music was limited, therefore, more particularly to its *sensuous* and *symbolic* side. The attention being exclusively directed to these factors, this concentration naturally developed them into effect-producing media of considerable strength—nay, of great subtlety. The music of the present day knows just as little of the prodigious elaboration of the

musical material, going the length of using even
"demi-semitones," and "the enharmonic family of
sound," as of the specific character of each individual
key and its close adaptation to the words both
spoken and sung. These subtle relations within
their narrow sphere, moreover, were destined for the
appreciation of a much more sensitive *audience*.
Just as the Greek ear was able to perceive infinitely
finer differences of interval than ours, exposed as it is
to a constantly varying temperature, so those races
were by nature far more susceptible and fonder of
emotional changes wrought by music than are we,
who take a meditative delight in the ingenious forms
which music conjures up, a delight which tends to
paralyze the elemental influence of sound. There
is no difficulty, therefore, in comprehending why
the action of music was more intense in ancient
times.

The same applies to a small number of those
anecdotes which record the specific effects produced
by the several *modes* of the Greeks. Their explanation is to be found in the scrupulous isolation
of the various modes, each mode being selected for
a definite purpose to the complete exclusion of any
alien admixture. The Doric mode was employed on
solemn, and particularly on religious occasions; by
means of the Phrygian the Greeks fired their armies
with courage; the Lydian signified mourning and
sadness; while wherever the Eolian resounded love-
making and banqueting was the order of the day.
This rigid and conventional division into four
principal modes, answering to as many states of

mind, and the circumstance that no poem was
ever recited *to any but its corresponding mode,* could
not but give to the mind a decided tendency to recall
at the sounds of a certain musical mode the feeling
associated with it. As a result of this one-sided
culture music had become an indispensable and docile
accessory of all the arts, a means for the attainment
of educational, political, and other ends ; it was a
maid-of-all-work but not a self-subsistent *art.* If the
strains of Phrygian music sufficed to incite warriors
to acts of bravery, if the faithfulness of grass-widows
could be secured by Doric songs, let generals and
husbands lament the extinction of the Greek system—
students of æsthetics and composers will cast no
regrets after it.

This morbid sensitiveness, in our opinion, is in
direct opposition to the *voluntary* and pure act of
contemplation which alone is the true and artistic
method of listening. Compared to it the ecstasies of
the musical enthusiast sink to the level of the crude
emotion of the savage. The beautiful is not
*suffered* but *enjoyed,* and the term "æsthetic enjoyment" clearly confirms this fact. Sentimentalists
regard it, of course, as heresy against the omnipotence
of music to take exception to the emotional revolutions
and conflicts which they discover in every musical
composition, and of which they never fail to experience
the full force. Those who cannot agree with them
are "callous," "apathetic," "cold reasoners." No
matter. It is, nevertheless, both ennobling and
elevating to follow the creative mind as it unlocks
with magic keys a new world of elements, and to

observe how at its bidding they enter into all conceivable combinations ; how it builds up and casts
down, creates and destroys, controlling the whole
wealth of an art which exalts the ear to an organ of
sense of the greatest delicacy and perfection. That
which calls forth from us a sympathetic response is
not in the least the passion professed to be described.
With a willing mind, calm but acutely sensitive,
we enjoy the work of art as it passes before us and
thoroughly realise the meaning of what Schelling so
felicitously terms "the sublime indifference of
Beauty."* Thus to enjoy with a keenly observant
mind is the most dignified and salutary mode,
and by no means the easiest one, of listening to
music.

The most important factor in the mental process
which accompanies the act of listening to music, and
which converts it into a source of pleasure, is
frequently overlooked. We here refer to the intellectual satisfaction which the listener derives from
continually following and anticipating the composer's
intentions—now, to see his expectations fulfilled,
and now, to find himself agreeably mistaken. It is a
matter of course that this intellectual flux and
reflux, this perpetual giving and receiving takes place
unconsciously, and with the rapidity of lightning-
flashes. Only *that* music can yield truly æsthetic
enjoyment which prompts and rewards the act of
thus closely following the composer's thoughts, and
which with perfect justice may be called *a pondering*

---

*" Ueber das Verhältniss der bildenden Künste zur Natur."

*of the imagination.* Indeed, without mental activity no æsthetic enjoyment is possible. But the kind of mental activity alluded to is quite peculiar to *music,* because its products, instead of being fixed and presented to the mind at once in their completeness, develop gradually and thus do not permit the listener to linger at any point, or to interrupt his train of thoughts. It demands, in fact, the keenest *watching* and the most untiring *attention.* In the case of intricate compositions, this may even become a mental exertion. Many an *individual,* nay, many a *nation* undertakes this exertion only with great reluctance. The monopoly of the soprano in the Italian School is mainly due to the mental indolence of the Italian people, who are incapable of that assiduous fixing of the attention so characteristic of Northern races, when listening to, and enjoying a musical *chef d'œuvre,* with all its intricacies of harmony and counterpoint. On the other hand, those whose store of mental energy is but small are *more easily* gratified, and such musical topers can consume quantities of music from which the æsthetic mind would shrink with dismay.

*Mental* activity is a necessary concomitant in every æsthetic enjoyment and often varies very considerably in several individuals, listening to one and the same composition. In the case of sensual and emotional natures it may sink to a minimum, whereas in highly intellectual persons it alone may turn the scale. It is the latter type of mind which in our opinion comes nearest to the "*golden mean.*" To become intoxicated nothing but weakness is required, but truly *æsthetic listening* is an *art* in itself.*

The habit of revelling in sensations and emotions is generally limited to those who have not the preparatory knowledge for the æsthetic appreciation of *musical* beauty. With the technically uninitiated " the feelings " play a predominant part, while, in the case of the trained musician, they are quite in the background. The greater the æsthetic element in the listener's mind (just as in the work of art), the more it counterbalances purely sensuous influences. It is for this reason that the time-

---

* It is quite in keeping with W. Heinse's enthusiastic and dissolute nature, to subordinate to a vague emotional impression the positive attributes of musical beauty. He goes so far (in "Hildegard von Hohenthal") as to say: "True music . . . . invariably aims at " conveying to the listener the meaning of the words and the feelings " they express, and it discharges this function so well and pleasantly, " that we are almost unconscious of it (the music). Such music " endures for ever; it is so natural that *we cease to be conscious of it as* " *music*, and only catch the meaning of the words."

The æsthetic appreciation of music, however, is only possible when our mind is fully awake; when we are " conscious " of the music, and *perfectly realise* all its points of beauty. Heinse, to whose naturalism we must pay that tribute of admiration to which it is entitled, has been greatly overrated as a poet, and still more as a musician. In consequence of the paucity of original treatises on music, Heinse has gradually come to be regarded and quoted as one of the best writers on musical æsthetics. How could the fact ever be overlooked that, after a few appropriate remarks, there forthwith comes such a flood of platitudes and manifest errors, as to make us marvel at so extraordinary an absence of culture ? His want of technical knowledge is coupled with an unsound æsthetic judgment, of which his analyses of operas by Gluck, Jomelli, Traëtta, and others afford abundant proof. Instead of throwing any light on the subject of art, they contain scarcely anything but enthusiastic exclamations.

honoured axiom of the theorists : "Grave music
"excites a feeling of sadness, and lively music makes
"us merry," is not always correct.  If every shallow
Requiem, every noisy funeral march, and every
whining Adagio had the power to make us sad, who
would care to prolong his existence in such a world ?
A composition that looks us in the face with the
bright eyes of beauty would make us glad, though
its object were to picture all the woes of the age ;
but the obstreperous gaiety of a *Finale* by Verdi, or
a Quadrille by Musard, has not always had a
cheering effect on us.

The untrained amateur and the musical senti-
mentalist are wont to ask whether the music is gay
or mournful, whereas the instructed musician
enquires whether it is good or bad.  The shadow
cast by such questions plainly indicates the different
positions in which the querists stand towards the
source of light.

Although we assert that true æsthetic enjoyment
depends upon the musical merit of the composition,
it by no means follows that the simple call of a bugle
or the sounds of "yodelling" in the mountains may
not at times afford us much greater delight than the
most exquisite Symphony.  But in cases such as
these *music comes under the head of the unassisted charms
of Nature as distinguished from art.*  The impression is
not produced by *this particular combination* of sounds
but by this special kind of *natural action,* and in point
of force it may, in conjunction with the rural beauty
of the surroundings and the individual frame of mind,
eclipse any æsthetic enjoyment whatsoever.  The

purely elemental may, therefore, preponderate over
the artistic.   Yet æsthetics, as the science of the
beautiful in art, can judge music only *in the sense of
an art* and can, therefore, take cognizance of nothing
but those effects which, as products of the human
mind, come within the scope of pure contemplation
in consequence of the definite grouping of the
primary factors.

Now the most essential condition to the æsthetic
enjoyment of music is that of listening to a composition *for its own sake*, no matter what it is or what
construction it may bear.   The moment music is
used as a means to induce certain states of mind, as
accessory or ornamental, it ceases to be an art in a
purely musical sense.   The *elemental properties* of
music are very frequently confounded with its *artistic*
beauty, in other words, a part is taken for the whole,
and unutterable confusion ensues.   Hundreds of
sayings about "music" do not apply to the art as
such, but to the sensuous action of its material only.

When Shakespeare's *Henry the Fourth* calls for
music on his deathbed (Part II., Act iv.), it is most
assuredly not to listen attentively to the performance,
but to lull himself with its ethereal elements, as in a
dream.   Nor are *Portia* and *Bassanio* ("Merchant of
Venice," Act III.) likely to have greatly heeded the
music which was being played during the ominous
choosing of the casket.   F. Strauss has composed
charming, nay, highly original music for his Waltzes,
but it ceases to be such when it is solely used to beat
time for the dancers.   In all these cases it is
utterly indifferent of what *quality* the music is, so long

as it has the fundamental character needed for the occasion, and wherever the question of individuality is a matter of indifference we get a *series of sounds,* but no *music.* Only he who carries away with him, not simply the vague after-effect of his feelings, but a definite and lasting impression of the *particular* composition, has truly heard and relished it. Those impressions which elevate our minds, and their supreme significance both in a psychical and a physiological sense, should not, however, hinder the art-critic from distinguishing in any given effect between its sensuous and its æsthetic element. From an æsthetic point of view music ought to be regarded as an effect rather than a cause, as a product rather than a producing agent.

Just as frequently as people confuse the elemental action of sound with music proper do they fail to distinguish the latter from the principles of rhythm and euphony, and from properties such as quiescence and motion, dissonance and consonance. The present state of music and philosophy forbid us, in the interest of both, to acquiesce in the expansion of the term " music " to the extent understood by the ancient Greeks, who used music in connection with all sciences and arts and the training of the mental faculties. The famous eulogy of music in " The Merchant of Venice " (V., i.)* is the result of such a confusion of ideas, music itself being confounded

---

* " The man that has no music in himself,
  Nor is not moved with concord of sweet sounds,
  Is fit for treasons, stratagems, and spoils," &c.

with its principles of euphony, consonance, and rhythm. In aphorisms of this kind we may, without greatly altering the sense, substitute for " music " such words as " poetry," " art "—nay, "beauty." The preference over the other arts, which *music* generally enjoys, is due to its somewhat questionable attribute of popularity. Proof of this is to be found in the immediately preceding verses of the quoted passage, which are full of praise of the soothing effect which music has on animals, thus making it once again play the part of a Van Aken.

The most instructive examples are to be met with in Bettina's " Musical Explosions," as Goethe politely styled her letters on music. Bettina, as the genuine type of a musical enthusiast, shows how improperly the meaning of the term "music" may be widened, in order to turn it freely to any use. Though ostensibly speaking of music, she always talks about the mysterious influence on her mind, and she wilfully incapacitates herself for a dispassionate investigation by luxuriating in the dreams of a lively imagination. A musical composition she invariably regards as a kind of natural product, and not as a creation of the human mind. She, therefore, always understands music only in a purely phenomenological sense. The terms, "music," "musical," Bettina applies to innumerable phenomena, simply because they happen to have one attribute or another in common with music, such as euphony, rhythm, and the power of exciting emotions. The question, however, does not turn on these isolated factors, but on the specific mode in which they are combined, and through which they are elevated to the rank of an art.  It is a matter of course that this romantic lady considers Goethe, nay, Christ Himself, as great musicians, though nobody knows whether the latter was one, and everybody knows that the former was not.

We respect historical modes of viewing things and the right of poetic licence, and can quite understand why Aristophanes, in his " Wasps," applies the epithets " wise and musical " (σοφὸν καὶ μουσικόν) to a highly-cultured mind.   Count Reinhardt's saying, too, that Oehlenschläger had " musical eyes " is very significant.   In scientific enquiries, however, we must exclude from the term " music " any but its æsthetic meaning, unless we are to abandon all hope ever to establish this protean science on firm ground.

# CHAPTER VI.

To view a thing in its relation to Nature is a proceeding of prime importance, and one likely to lead to most momentous results. Whoever has even slightly felt the pulse of the times, knows that this conviction is rapidly gaining ground. In all modern research there is a strong leaning to study phenomena by the light of the laws of nature, so that enquiries even into the most abstruse subjects gravitate perceptibly towards the method obtaining in the natural sciences. The science of *æsthetics*, too, unless it be satisfied with a sort of sham existence, ought to know the knotty root as well as the delicate fibre by which every individual art is connected with the natural order of things. Now, the relation subsisting between music and Nature discloses the most pregnant truths in respect of musical æsthetics, and on the just appreciation of this relation depends the treatment of its most difficult subjects and the solution of its most debatable points.

Art—considered, first of all, as passive, not as active—stands in a twofold relation to surrounding Nature : primarily, in respect of the crude matter from which it produces ; and secondly, in respect of the forms of beauty which the external world affords it for artistic reproduction. In both cases, Nature stands to art in the position of a kindly benefactress, by supplying the most vital and essential requirements.  It must now be our endeavour to quickly review these resources in the interest of musical æsthetics, and to enquire what share of the rational, and, therefore, unequal gifts of Nature has fallen to the lot of music.

On examining in what sense Nature provides music with its *material*, we find that she supplies nothing but the rough elements, from which man contrives to elicit sounds.  The silent ore of the mountains, the wood of the forest, the skin and gut of animals, is all that constitutes the raw material, properly so-called, with which the *musical note* is formed.  At the outset, therefore, we are furnished only with material for the production of material, that is, of sound of high or low pitch; in other words, the measurable tone.  The latter is the primary and essential condition of all music, whose function it is to so combine these tones as to produce *melody* and *harmony*, its two main factors.  Neither of them is provided for us by Nature ready made, but both are creations of the human mind.

The systematic succession of measurable tones which we call *melody* is not to be met with in Nature, even in its most rudimentary form.  Sound-phenomena in unassisted Nature present no intelligible proportions, nor can they be reduced to our scale.  Melody, on the other hand, is the " initial force," the life-blood, the primitive cell of the musical organism, with which the drift and development of the composition are closely bound up.

Just as little as melody, do we find in Nature—the sublime harmony of its phenomena notwithstanding—

*harmony* in a musical sense, the simultaneous occurrence of certain notes. Has anybody ever heard a triad, a chord of the sixth or the seventh in Nature? Harmony like melody is an achievement of man, only belonging to a much later period.

The Greeks knew of no harmony, but sang in octaves or in unison, just as do at the present time those Asiatic tribes who are known to sing. The use of *dissonances* (among which we must include *the third and the sixth*) came gradually into vogue in the twelfth century, while as late as the fifteenth century, to effect modulations, the octave only was used. All the intervals which our present system of harmony puts into requisition had to be discovered one by one, and often more than a century was needed for so insignificant an acquisition. Neither the race that most cultivated art in ancient times, nor the most erudite composers of the early part of the Middle Ages were able to do what our shepherdesses of the most out-of-the-way mountains can do at the present day—to sing in thirds. It must not be supposed, however, that the introduction of harmony was an *additional* source of light to music, for it was through harmony that the art first emerged from utter darkness. " Music, properly so-called, was not born until then " (Nägeli).

We have seen that Nature is destitute both of melody and harmony; but there is a third factor regulating the two former, which existed prior to man, and is consequently not of his creation. This factor is *rhythm*. In the galloping of the horse, the

K

clack of the mill, the singing of the blackbird and the quail, there is an element of periodically recurring motion in the successive beats which, when looked at in the aggregate, blend into an intelligible whole. Not all, yet many sounds in Nature are rhythmical, and in these the principle of *duple-time rhythm* (manifesting itself in the rise and fall, the ebb and flow) is invariably discernible. But the point in which natural rhythm differs from human music is obvious: in *music* there is no independent rhythm; it occurs only in connection with melody and harmony expressed in rhythmical order. Rhythm in Nature, on the other hand, is associated neither with melody nor harmony, but is perceptible only in aerial vibrations, that cannot be reduced to a definite quantity. It is the only musical element which Nature possesses, the first we are conscious of, and that with which the mind of the infant and the savage becomes soonest familiar. When South Sea Islanders rattle with wooden staves and pieces of metal to the accompaniment of fearful howlings, they are performing *natural* music, that is, *no music at all*. But what a Tyrolese peasant sings, though apparently uninfluenced by art-culture, is, beyond dispute, *artificial* music. The man fancies, of course, that he sings as Nature prompts him, but to enable Nature so to prompt him, the seed of centuries had to grow and ripen.

We have now examined the elements which form the groundwork of the music of to-day, and have been forced to the conclusion that man has not learnt it from surrounding Nature. The manner and sequence in which music developed into our present system is a subject treated in the history of music.   Here it is enough to take the facts for granted and to emphasize the conclusions arrived at—namely, that melody and harmony, our intervals and our scale, the division into major and minor, according to the position of the semitone, and lastly, the equal temperament without which our music (the West European) would be impossible, are slowly gained triumphs of the human mind.   Nature has given man but the organs and the inclination to sing, together with the faculty to create a musical system, having its roots in the most simple relations of sound.   Only the latter (the triad, harmonic progression) will ever remain the indestructible foundation upon which all future development must rest.   Let us keep clear of the error, that *this* (the present) *musical system* is itself an inherent element in Nature.   Although even scientists now-a-days manipulate musical relations, to all appearance, without any difficulty, as though the power to do so were innate, this by no means proves our present musical laws ᵗo be so many laws of Nature, but is simply due to the enormous spread of musical culture.   Hand, therefore, is quite right in remarking that our infants in the cradle sing better than adult savages. " If the succession of musical notes were a necessary " product of Nature, everybody would sing in tune."*

---

* Hand (Æsthetik der Tonkunst, I., 50) also very justly directs attention to the fact that the musical scales of the Scotch Gaels and the various tribes of India are alike in the peculiarity of having neither fourth nor seventh, the succession of their notes being C, D, E, G, A, C.   The physically well-developed Patagonians in

If we apply the term "artificial" to our musical system, it must not be construed into the subtilised meaning of an arbitrary and conventional arrangement, but as signifying something that has gradually developed, as distinguished from something pre-existing in a complete form.

Hauptmann overlooks this distinction, when he calls the notion of an artificial system of music an " absolutely empty one, because musicians were just " as powerless to devise intervals and a musical " system, as philologists to invent the words and " the construction of a language."* Language is an artificial product in precisely the same sense as music, since neither exists ready prepared in Nature, but both have been formed by degrees and have to be specially learnt. Languages are not framed by philologists, but by the nations themselves according to their idiosyncrasies, and by way of perfecting them, modifications are continually introduced. In the same way " musical philologists " have not laid the "foundation " of music, but have merely fixed and substantiated what generations of musical talents have unconsciously brought forth with rational consistency, though not with inherent necessity.†

---

South America are entirely ignorant of both vocal and instrumental music. Our above conclusions, moreover, are amply confirmed by the recent and exhaustive enquiries of Helmholtz into the growth of our present system of music (" Lehre von den Tonempfindungen").

* M. Hauptmann, "Die Natur der Harmonik und Metrik," 1853, p. 7.

† Our view accords with the researches of Jacob Grimm, who among other things remarks: " Whoever has gained the conviction " that language has originated in the alembic of the human mind, will " have no doubt as to the source of poetry and music." (" Ursprung " der Sprache," 1852.)

From this process of evolution we may infer that our musical system will also, in course of time, be enriched with new forms and undergo further changes. Music within its present limits, however, is still capable of such great development, that an alteration in the nature of the system seems a very remote contingency as yet. If, for instance, the system were widened by the "emancipation of the demi-semitones" (of which a modern authoress professes to have found adumbrations in Chopin's music)* the theories of harmony, composition, and musical æsthetics would become totally changed. The musical theorist may, therefore, at present, indulge in this glimpse into the future only so far as to concede the bare possibility of such changes.

To disprove our assertion that there is no music in Nature, the wealth of sound that enlivens her is generally cited as counter-evidence. Should not the murmuring brook, the roar of the ocean waves, the thundering avalanche, and the howling of the wind be at once the source of, and the model for human music? Have all these rippling, whistling, and roaring noises nothing to do with our system of music? We have no option but to reply in the negative. All such sounds are *mere noise*—*i.e.*, an irregular succession of sonorous pulses. Very seldom, and even then only in an isolated manner, does Nature bring forth a *musical note* of definite and

---

* Johanna Kinkel, "Acht Briefe über Clavierunterricht," 1852 (Cotta).

measurable pitch. But a musical note is the foundation of all music. However deeply and agreeably these natural sounds may affect the mind, they form no stepping stone to human music, but are mere elemental semblances of it, though it is true, that eventually they may, for the mature human music, become highly suggestive factors. Even the purest phenomenon in the natural world of sound, the song of birds, has no relation to music, as it cannot be reduced to our scale. Natural harmony, too, —certainly the sole and indestructible basis existing in Nature, on which the principal relations of our music repose—should be viewed in its true light. Harmonic progression on the Æolian harp (an instrument with all its strings alike) is produced by the spontaneous action of Nature, and is grounded, therefore, on some natural law; but the progression itself is not the immediate product of Nature. Unless a certain measurable, fundamental tone be sounded on a musical instrument, there can be no auxiliary tones and consequently no harmonic progression. Man must ask before Nature can reply. The reflection of sound, called echo, is susceptible of a still simpler explanation. It is a singular fact, that even authors of great ability fail to recognise the fallacy that there is *real music* in Nature. Hand himself, whom we have intentionally quoted before, to testify to his accurate judgment respecting the incommensurableness and the inapplicability of natural sounds for purposes of art, devotes a special chapter to " music in nature," of which the sonorous waves might " in a manner " also be called music. Krüger expresses himself similarly.* But when it is a question of first principles, saving clauses such as "in a manner" are wholly inadmissible: the sounds we hear in Nature either are, or are not, music. The criterion can only be the measurableness of the tone. Hand continually emphasizes "the inspiration," "the revealing of the inner man" and of a "subjective feeling," "the force of individual energy, through "which the inmost thoughts find direct utterance." According to this principle the singing of birds ought to be called music, whereas the tune of a musical box ought not to be called so. Yet the very opposite is the truth.

The "music" of Nature and the music of man belong to two distinct categories. The transition from the former to the latter passes through the science of *mathematics*. An important and pregnant proposition. Still, we should be wrong were we to construe it in the sense that man framed his musical system according to calculations purposely made, the system having arisen through the unconscious application of pre-existent conceptions of quantity and proportion, through subtle processes of measuring and counting; but the laws by which the latter are governed were demonstrated only subsequently by science.

As everything in music must be measurable, while the spontaneous sounds of Nature cannot be reduced to any definite quantity, these two realms of sound have no true point of contact. Nature does not

---

* "Beiträge für Leben und Wissenschaft der Tonkunst," page 149, &c.

supply us with the art-elements of a complete and
ready prepared system of sound, but only with the
crude matter which we utilise for our music.   Not
the voices of animals, but their gut is of importance
to us; and the animal to which music is most
indebted is not the nightingale, but the sheep.

After this preliminary enquiry, which for the
just appreciation of the musically beautiful is but
the basement, indispensable though it be, we will
pass onward to a higher region, to the domain of
æsthetics.

The measurable tone and the complete system
are merely the means *with which* the composer
produces, not *what* he produces.   As wood and ore
are but "matter" in respect of the tone, so the
tone is but "matter" in respect of music.   But
there is a third and higher sense of the term
"matter": matter in the sense of the subject to be
treated—the idea to be conveyed—the theme.
Whence does the composer derive the matter thus
understood?   Whence arise the contents of any
given composition, the subject which gives it its
individual and distinctive character?

*Poetry, painting,* and *sculpture* possess in surrounding Nature an inexhaustible store of subject-
matter.   The poet or artist here is impressed by
some *beautiful object in Nature* which forthwith
becomes the subject of some original production.

The function of Nature to supply art with models
is most strikingly exemplified in *painting* and
*sculpture*.   The painter could draw no tree, no
flower, if they did not already exist in the external

world ; the sculptor could produce no statue without
knowing the human form, and without using it as a
model.  The same holds good of ideal subjects.  In
the strict sense of the word they are not " ideal."
Is not the " ideal " landscape composed of rocks,
trees, water, drifts of cloud—of things, in brief,
which occur in Nature ?  The painter can paint
nothing but what he has *seen* and closely observed,
no matter whether he paints a landscape, a " genre,"
or a historical painting.  When our contemporaries
paint " Huss," " Luther," or " Egmont," though
they have never actually beheld their subject, its
component parts cannot have been copied but from
Nature.  The painter need not necessarily have
seen *this very man*, but he must have seen a great
number of men moving, standing, and walking ; he
must have noticed their appearance when illuminated or when casting shadows.  The impossibility
or unreality of the painter's figures would assuredly
be his greatest reproach.

*Poetry*, which Nature furnishes with a far wider
range of beautiful models, is in an analogous
position.  Man and his deeds, his feelings and suffer-
ings, as coming under our own observation, or as
handed down to us by tradition—for tradition, too, is
a pre-existing factor, something which the poet finds
already supplied—are the subject-matter of the
poem, the tragedy, the novel.  The poet can give
us no description of a sunrise, a snow-field, or an
emotion ; he can introduce neither peasant, soldier,
miser, nor lover into his play, without having seen
or studied their originals in Nature, or without being

enabled by accurate accounts to form in his own mind such vivid images of them as compensate for the want of having them actually present.

Now, on comparing *music* with those arts, it is obvious that Nature has provided no model capable of becoming its subject-matter.

*There is nothing beautiful in Nature as far as music is concerned.*

This distinction between music and the other arts (with the sole exception of *architecture*, which is likewise without models in Nature) is a profound and momentous one.

The work of the painter or poet is a continual copying or reproducing (drawn from reality or the imagination), but it is impossible to *copy music* from Nature.   Nature knows of no Sonata, no Overture, no Rondo ; but she knows of landscapes, of scenes of every-day life, of idyls and tragedies.   The Aristotelian proposition, that it is the office of art to imitate Nature—a proposition which philosophers even of the last century viewed with favour—has long since been amended, and, having been commented upon *ad nauseam*, it needs no further exposition in this enquiry.   Art should not slavishly copy Nature, but *remodel* it.   This expression alone shows that something must have existed *prior* to art that admits of being remodelled.   This something is the prototype, the thing of beauty which Nature provides for art.   A beautiful landscape, a group, or a poem inspires the painter to an artistic reproduction ; while the poet is similarly inspired by a historical event, or by some adventure.   But what is there in Nature that could ever induce the *composer* to exclaim : what a magnificent model for an Overture, a Symphony !   The composer can *remodel* nothing; he has to create everything *ab initio.* That which the painter or the poet gleans in contemplating the beautiful in Nature, the composer has to draw from his own fertile imagination.   He must watch for the propitious moment, when it begins to ring and sing within him ; he will then enter heart and soul into his task, and create from within that which has not its like in Nature, and which, therefore, unlike the other arts, is truly not of this world.

If, in respect of the painter and the poet, we classed *man* with the " beautiful objects " in Nature, whereas in respect of the composer we excluded the rich melodies of man in their pristine freshness, we did not do so from bias.   The singing shepherd is not an object, but a subject of our art.   His song, if consisting of measurable and systematically adjusted successions of notes, how simple soever these may be, is a creation of the human mind, no matter whether a herdboy or a Beethoven invented it.

A composer who introduces into his music true national airs does not thereby make use of a spontaneous product of Nature, the airs being always traceable to someone who originated them—how did he come by them ?  Did he copy them from a model in Nature ?  This is the question we must ask, and only a negative reply is possible.   Popular airs are not things already existing—natural objects of beauty, as it were—but they are the first stage of true art,

*art in its native simplicity.* Such airs are natural
models for music just as little as the flowers and
soldiers daubed with charcoal on the walls of guard-
rooms and lumber yards are natural models for
painting. Both are products of human art. Of the
figures drawn in charcoal the originals exist in
Nature, whereas for the popular air no such original
exists; it cannot be traced to any prototype in nature.

A very common error arises from the term
"subject" being understood in its wider sense when
speaking of music, in support of which it is pointed
out that Beethoven really composed an Overture to
"Egmont" or (to avoid reminding us by the pre-
position "to" of its dramatic meaning) that Beethoven
composed "Egmont," Berlioz "King Lear," and
Mendelssohn "Melusina." Have not these narratives,
say they, furnished the composer with subjects, as
they do the poet? Not in the least. To the poet
these characters are true models which he recasts,
whereas to the composer they are mere *suggestions*—
*i.e., poetic* suggestions. The natural model for the
composer would have to be an *audible* something, as
it is a visible something for the painter and a
tangible something for the sculptor. The individuality
of "Egmont," his deeds, experiences, and sentiments,
do not form the subject of Beethoven's Overture, as
they do in the case of the painting or the drama
"Egmont." The subject of the Overture consists of
*successions of notes*, which the composer drew from the
store of his own imagination, free from all limitations,
except those fixed by the intrinsic laws of music.
These successions of notes are, æsthetically speaking,

entirely independent of the idea "Egmont" with
which the poetic fancy of the composer alone has
linked them ; no matter whether this idea first
suggested them in some inscrutable manner, or
whether he subsequently found them suitable for his
composition.   This connection, however, is so loose
and arbitrary that in listening to a piece of music we
should never even guess at its alleged subject, but for
the name purposely attached to it by the author.  It is
*this name* alone which, from the very beginning, forces
our thoughts into a certain channel.   Berlioz's
magnificent Overture is no more causally related
to the idea " King Lear" than a Waltz by Strauss.
It is impossible to lay too much stress upon this
fact, as the most erroneous views prevail on this very
point.   Only on *comparing* the Waltz by Strauss
or the Overture by Berlioz with the idea " King
Lear," does the former appear to be inconsistent
and the latter consistent with it.   But we are induced
to make the comparison by the explicit command of
the author, and not by something inherent in the
music itself.   A certain title prompts us to contrast
the piece of music with some object external to it,
and we are thus under the necessity of measuring it
by some standard *other* than the *musical* one.

It may possibly be said that Beethoven's Overture
to " Prometheus " is not sufficiently grand for the
subject, but intrinsically it is proof against all attacks,
and nowhere can a musical flaw or imperfection
be shown to exist.   The Overture is perfect because
the working out of its *musical* subject is faultless.
To treat its *poetic* part in like manner is a totally

different matter. The poetic treatment arises and disappears with the title. In the case of a composition with a definite title, this demand can, moreover, only apply to certain characteristic attributes: the music may have to be solemn or lively, gloomy or cheerful; its opening may have to be simple and its close gay or mournful, &c. Poetry and painting are expected to clothe their subjects in a definite and concrete individuality, and not merely with general attributes. For this reason it is quite conceivable that Beethoven's Overture to "Egmont" would bear equally well the title "William Tell" or "Joan of Arc." But the *drama* "Egmont," or the *painting* "Egmont" could at the worst only lead to the error that another individual in the same position is meant, but not that the circumstances themselves are entirely different.

It is clear, therefore, that the relation of music to Nature is most intimately connected with the question of its *subject-matter.*

There is still another factor selected from musical literature, for the purpose of proving that music has a prototype in Nature. Instances are adduced of composers having derived from Nature not only their poetic inspiration (as in the cases alluded to), but of having faithfully reproduced some of her spontaneous utterances: the cock-crowing in Haydn's Oratorio "The Seasons," the call of the cuckoo, the song of the nightingale, the whistle of the quail in Beethoven's "Pastoral" Symphony and in Spohr's "Consecration of Sound." But though we *recognise* these imitations, and though we *listen*

to them in a *musical* work, their meaning is a poetic
and not a musical one.  The cock-crowing is not
introduced as *beautiful* music, or indeed as music at
all, but merely to recall in us the impression associated in our mind with the phenomenon in question.
" I have almost *seen* Haydn's ' Creation,' " wrote
Thieriot to Jean Paul, after listening to a performance of this Oratorio.  We are only reminded
by universally-known sayings and quotations that it
is early morn, a balmy summer's night, or spring-
time.  Except in a purely descriptive sense, no
composer has ever been able to utilise the sounds of
Nature for any truly musical purpose.  All the
natural sounds in the world are powerless to produce
a single musical *theme*, simply because they are *not
music*, and it is significant that music can only enlist
Nature into its service, if it wants to dabble in the
art of painting.*

---

* The misconception that the spontaneous sounds of Nature should
be bodily transferred to a musical composition—which, as O. Jahn
aptly remarks, is admissible only in rare cases as a jest, is a totally
different thing from such cases (which, by the way, ought not to be
called "painting" at all) where semi-musical phenomena, through
their rhythmic or sonorous character,—*e.g.*, the rushing and splashing
of water, the singing of birds, the howling of the wind, the whizzing
of arrows, the humming of the spinning-wheel, &c., suggest to the
composer—but are by no means "literally copied " by him—themes
of independent beauty, which are worked out with perfect freedom
and bear the impress of true art.  " Of this privilege the poet makes
" use in the choice of the words and the metre; but in music it extends
" over a much wider area, countless musical elements being scattered
"throughout Nature," and an abundance of notable examples is
supplied both by classical and modern composers; only the latter
proceed with much greater subtlety than did the former.

## CHAPTER VII.

HAS Music any subject? This has been a burning question ever since people began to reflect upon music. It has been answered both in the affirmative and in the negative. Many prominent men, almost exclusively *philosophers*, among whom we may mention Rousseau, Kant, Hegel, Herbart,* Kahlert, &c., hold that music has no subject. The numerous physiologists who endorse this view include such eminent thinkers as Lotze and Helmholtz, whose opinions, strengthened as they are by musical knowledge, carry great weight and authority. Those who contend that music *has a subject* are numerically far stronger : among them are the trained *musicians* of the literary profession, and their convictions are shared by the bulk of the public.

It may seem almost a matter for surprise that just those who are familiar with the technical side of music should be unwilling to concede the untenableness of a doctrine which is at variance with those very technical principles, and which thinkers on abstract subjects might perhaps be pardoned for

---

* Robert Zimmermann, in his recent work, " Die allgemeine Æsthetik als Formwissenschaft " (Vienna, 1865), founded as it is on Herbart's principles, has applied the morphological principle with strict logical consistency to all arts, and consequently also to music.

propounding. The reason is, that many of these musical authors are more anxious to save the so-called honour of their art than to ascertain the truth. They attack the doctrine that music has no subject, not as one opinion against another, but as heresy against dogma. The contrary view appears to them in the light of a degrading error and a form of crude and heinous materialism. " What! the art that "charms and elevates us; to which so many noble " minds have devoted a whole lifetime; which is the " vehicle of the most sublime thoughts; *that* art to " be cursed with unmeaningness, to be mere food for " the senses, mere empty sound!" Hackneyed exclamations of this description which, though made up of several disconnected propositions, are generally uttered in one breath, neither prove nor disprove anything. The question is not a point of honour, not a party-badge, but simply the discovery of truth; and in order to attain this object, it is of the first importance to be clear regarding the points which are under debate.

It is the indiscriminate use of the terms, *contents, subject, matter*, which has been, and still is, responsible for all this ambiguity; the same meaning being expressed by different terms, or the same term associated with different meanings. "*Contents*," in the true and original sense, is that which a thing *contains*, what it holds within. The *notes* of which a piece of music is composed, and which are the parts that go to make up the whole, are the contents in this sense. The circumstance that nobody will accept this

L

definition as a satisfactory solution, but that it is dis-
missed as a truism, is due to the word "contents"
(subject) being usually confounded with the word
"object." An enquiry into the "contents" of
musical compositions raises in such people's minds
the conception of an "*object*" (subject-matter ;
topic), which latter, being the idea, the ideal element,
they represent to themselves as almost antithetical
to the "material part," the musical notes. Music
has, indeed, no contents as thus understood ; no
*subject* in the sense that the subject to be treated is
something extraneous to the musical notes. Kahlert
is right in emphatically maintaining that music,
unlike painting, admits of no " description in words "
(Æsth. 380), though his subsequent assumption
that a description in words may, at times, " compensate for the want of æsthetic enjoyment," is false.
It may be the means, however, of clearly perceiving
the real bearing of the question. The query
"what" is the subject of the music, must necessarily
be answerable in words, if music really has a
" *subject,*" because an " indefinite subject " upon
which everyone puts a different construction, which
can only be felt and not translated into words, is not
a subject as we have defined it.

Music consists of successions and forms of sound,
and these alone constitute the subject. They again
remind us of architecture and dancing which likewise aim at beauty in form and motion, and are also
devoid of a definite subject. Now, whatever be the
effect of a piece of music on the individual mind, and
howsoever it be interpreted, it has no *subject* beyond

the combinations of notes we hear, for music does not only speak *by means of sounds*, it speaks nothing but *sound*.

Krüger—the opponent of Hegel and Kahlert—who is probably the most learned advocate of the doctrine that music has a " subject "—contends that this art presents but a different side of the subject which other arts, such as painting, represent. " All plastic figures," he says (Beiträge, 131), " are in a state of " quiescence ; they do not exhibit present, but past " action, or the state of things at a given moment. " The painting, therefore, does not show Apollo van- " quishing, but it represents the victor, the furious " warrior," &c. Music, on the other hand, "supplies to " those plastic and quiescent forms the motive force, " the active principle, the inner waves of motion; and " whereas in the former instance we knew the true, " but inert subject, to be anger, love, &c., we here " know the true and active subject to be loving, rush- " ing, heaving, storming, fuming." The latter portion is only partly true, for though music may be said to " rush, heave, and storm," it can neither " love " nor be "angry." These sentiments we ourselves import into the music, and we must here refer our readers to the second chapter of this book. Krüger then proceeds to compare the definiteness of the *painter's subject* with the *musical subject*, and remarks : "The " *painter* represents Orestes, pursued by the Furies : " his outward appearance, his eyes, mouth, forehead, " and posture, give us the impression of flight, gloom, " and despair; at his heels the spirits of divine " vengeance, whose imperious and sublimely terrible

" commands he cannot evade, but who likewise present
" unchanging outlines, features, and attitudes.  The
" *composer* does not exhibit fleeing Orestes in fixed
" lines, but from a point of view from which the
" painter cannot pourtray him : he puts into his music
" the tremor and shuddering of his soul, his inmost
" feelings at war, urging his flight," &c.  This, in our
opinion, is entirely false ; the composer is unable to
represent Orestes either in one way or another; in
fact, *he cannot represent him at all.*

The objection that sculpture and painting are also
unable to represent to us a given historical
personage, and that we could not know the figure to
be *this very* individual, but for our previous knowledge
of certain historical facts, does not hold good.
True, the figure does not proclaim itself to be
Orestes; the man who has gone through such or
such experiences, and whose existence is bound up
with certain biographic incidents ; none but the *poet*
can represent that, since he alone can narrate the
events; but the painting " Orestes " unequivocally
shows us a youth with noble features, in Greek
attire, his looks and attitude betokening fear and
mental anguish ; and it shows us this youth pursued
and tormented by the awe-inspiring goddesses of
vengeance.  All this is clear and indubitable ; a
visible narrative—no matter whether the youth be
called Orestes or otherwise.  Only the antecedent
causes—namely, that the youth has committed
matricide, &c., cannot be expressed.  Now, what can
music give us in point of definiteness as a counterpart to the visible subject of the painter—apart

from the historical element? Chords of a diminished
seventh, themes in minor keys, a rolling bass, &c.—
musical forms, in brief, which might signify a woman
just as well as a youth; one pursued by myrmidons
instead of furies; somebody tortured by jealousy or
by bodily pain; one bent on revenge—in short, anything we can think of, if we must needs imagine a
subject for the composition.

It seems almost superfluous to expressly recall the
proposition, already established by us, that whenever
the subject and the descriptive power of music are
under debate, *instrumental music* alone can be taken
into account. Nobody is likely to disregard this so
far as to instance Orestes in Gluck's "Iphigenia,"
for this "Orestes" is not the *composer's* creation.
The words of the poet, the appearance and gestures
of the actor, the costume and the painter's decora-
tions produce the complete Orestes. The composer's contribution—the melody—is possibly the
most *beautiful* part of all, but it happens to be just
that factor which has nothing whatever to do with
the real Orestes.

Lessing has shown with admirable perspicuity
what the poet and what the sculptor or painter may
make of the story of Laocoon. The poet by the
aid of speech gives us the historical, individually-
defined Laocoon; the painter and sculptor shows us
the terrible serpents, crushing in their coils an old
man and two boys (of determinate age and appearance, dressed after a particular fashion, &c.), who
by their looks, attitudes, and gestures express the
agonies of approaching death. Of the *composer*

Lessing says nothing, and this was only to be
expected, since there is nothing in "Laocoon"
which could be turned into music.

We have already alluded to the intimate connection between the question of *subject* in musical
compositions and the relation of music to the
*beauties of Nature.* The composer looks in vain for
models such as those which render the subjects of
other art-products both definite and recognisable,
and an art for which Nature can provide no æsthetic
model must, properly speaking, be incorporeal. A
prototype of its mode of manifestation is nowhere
to be met with, and it can, therefore, not be included in the range of living experiences. It does
not reproduce an already known and classified
subject, and for this reason it has no subject that
can be taken hold of by the intellect, as the latter
can be exercised only on definite conceptions.

The term *subject* (substance) can, properly
speaking, be applied to an art-product only, if we
regard it as the correlative of *form.* The terms
"form" and "substance" supplement each other,
and one cannot be thought of except in relation to
the other. Wherever the "form" appears mentally
inseparable from the "substance," there can be no
question of an independent "substance" (subject).
Now, in music, substance and form, the subject and
its working out, the image and the realised conception are mysteriously blended in one undecomposable whole. This complete fusion of substance and
form is exclusively characteristic of music, and
presents a sharp contrast to poetry, painting, and

sculpture, inasmuch as these arts are capable of representing the same idea and the same event in different forms.  The story of William Tell supplied to Florian the subject for a historical novel, to Schiller the subject for a play, while Goethe began to treat it as an epic poem.  The substance is everywhere the same, equally resolvable into prose, and capable of being narrated; always clearly recognisable, and yet the form differs in each case. Aphrodite emerging from the sea is the subject of innumerable paintings and statues, the various forms of which it is, nevertheless, impossible to confuse.  In music, no distinction can be made between substance and form, as it has no form independently of the substance.  Let us look at this more closely.

In all compositions the independent, æsthetically undecomposable subject of a musical conception is the *theme*, and by the theme, the musical microcosm, we should always be able to test the alleged subject underlying the music as such.  Let us examine the leading theme of some composition, say that of Beethoven's Symphony in B flat major.  What is its subject (substance)?  What its form?  Where does the latter commence and the former end? That its subject does not consist of a determinate feeling, we think we have conclusively proved, and this truth becomes only the more evident when tested by this or by any other concrete example. What then is to be called its *subject?*  The groups of sounds?  Undoubtedly; but they have a form already.  And what is the *form?*  The groups of

sounds again ; but here they are a *replete* form.
Every practical attempt at resolving a theme into
subject and form ends in arbitrariness and contradiction.  Take, for instance, a theme repeated by
another instrument or in the higher octave.  Is the
subject changed thereby or the form ?  If, as is
generally the case, the latter is said to be changed,
then all that remains as the *subject* of the theme
would simply be the series of intervals, the skeleton
frame for the musical notation as the score presents
them to the eye.  But this is not *musical* definiteness,
it is an abstract notion.  It may be likened to a
pavilion with stained window panes, through which
the same environment appears, now red, now blue,
and now yellow.  The environment itself changes
neither in *substance* nor in *form*, but merely in *colour*.
This property of exhibiting the same forms in
countless hues, from the most glaring contrasts down
to the finest distinctions of shade, is quite peculiar
to music and is one of the most fertile and powerful
causes of its effectiveness.

A theme originally composed for the piano and
subsequently arranged for the orchestra acquires
thereby a *new form* but not a *form for the first time*,
the formal element being part and parcel of the
primary conception.  The assertion that a theme by
the process of instrumentation changes its subject
while retaining its form is even less tenable, as such
a theory involves still greater contradictions, the
listener being obliged to affirm, that though he
recognises it to be the same subject "it somehow
"sounds like a different one."

It is true that in looking at a composition in the aggregate and more particularly at musical works of great length, we are in the habit of speaking of form and subject; in such a case, however, these terms are not understood in their primitive and logical sense, but in a specifically *musical* one. What we call the "form" of a Symphony, an Overture, a Sonata, an Aria, a Chorus, &c., is the architectonic combination of the units and groups of units of which a composition is made up; or more definitely speaking, the symmetry of their successions, their contrasts, repetitions, and general working out. But thus understood the subject is identical with the *themes* with which this architectonic structure is built up. Subject is here, therefore, no longer construed in the sense of an "object," but as the subject in a purely musical sense. The words "substance" and "form" in respect of entire compositions are used in an æsthetic, and not in a strictly logical sense. If we wish to apply them to music in the latter sense, we must do so, not in relation to the composition in the aggregate, as a whole consisting of parts, but in relation to its ultimate and æsthetically undecomposable idea. This ultimate idea is the *theme* or *themes*, and in the latter substance and form are indissolubly connected. We cannot acquaint anybody with the "subject" of a theme, *except by playing it*. The subject of a composition can, therefore, not be understood as an object derived from an external source, but as something intrinsically musical; in other words, as the concrete group of sounds in a piece of music. Now, as a composition must comply with the formal laws of beauty, it cannot run on arbitrarily and at random, but must develop gradually with intelligible and organic definiteness, as buds develop into rich blossoms.

Here we have the *principal theme;* the true topic or subject of the entire composition. Everything it contains, though originated by the unfettered imagination, is nevertheless the natural outcome and effect of the theme which determines and forms, regulates and pervades its every part. We may compare it to a self-evident truth which we accept for a moment as satisfactory, but which our mind would fain see tested and developed, and in the musical working out this development takes place analogously to the logical train of reasoning in an argument. The theme, not unlike the chief hero in a novel, is brought by the composer into the most varied states and surrounding conditions, and is made to pass through ever-changing phases and moods— everything, no matter what contrasts it may present, is conceived and formed in relation to the theme.

The epithet *without a subject,* might possibly be applied to the freest form of extemporising, during which the performer indulges in chords, arpeggios, and rosalias, by way of a rest, rather than as a creative effort, and which does not end in the production of a definite and connected whole. Such extempore playing has no individuality of its own, by which one might recognise or distinguish it, and it would be quite correct to say that it has no subject (in the wider sense of the term), because it has no theme.

Thus the theme or the themes are the real subject of a piece of music.

In æsthetic and critical reviews far too little importance is attached to the *leading theme* of a composition ; it alone reveals at once the mind which conceived the work. Every musician, on hearing the first few opening bars of Beethoven's Overture to " Leonore " or Mendelssohn's Overture to " The Hebrides," though he may be totally unaware of the subsequent development of the theme, must recognise at once the treasure that lies before him ; whereas the music of a theme from Donizetti's " Fausta " Overture or Verdi's Overture to " Louisa Miller " will, without the need of further examination, convince us that the music is fit only for low music halls. German theorists and executants prize the musical working-out far more than the inherent merits of the theme. But whatever is not contained in the theme (be it overtly or in disguise) is incapable of organic growth, and if the present time is barren of orchestral works of the Beethoven type it is, perhaps, due not so much to an imperfect knowledge of the working out, as to the want of symphonic power and fe ility of the *themes.*

On enquiring into the *subject* of music we should, above all, beware of using the term " subject " in a eulogistic sense. From the fact that music has no extrinsic subject (object) it does not follow that it is without any *intrinsic merit.* It is clear that those who, with the zeal of partisanship, contend that music has a " subject," really mean " intellectual merit." We can only ask our readers to revert to our remarks in the third chapter of this book. Music is to be played, but it is not to be played with. Thoughts and feelings pervade with vital energy the musical organism, the embodiment of beauty and symmetry, and though they are not identical with the *organism itself* nor yet *visible*, they are, as it were, its breath of life. The composer *thinks* and *works;* but he thinks and works in *sound*, away from the realities of the external world. We deliberately repeat this commonplace, for even those who admit it in principle, deny and violate it when carried to its logical conclusions. They conceive the act of composing as a translation into sound of a given subject, whereas the sounds themselves are the untranslatable and original tongue. If the composer is obliged to think in sounds, it follows as a matter of course that music has no subject external to itself, for of a subject in this sense we ought to be able to think in *words*.

Though, when examining into the *subject* of music, we rigorously excluded compositions written for given sets of words as being inconsistent with the conception of music pure and simple, yet the master-pieces of vocal music are indispensable for the formation of an accurate judgment respecting the *intrinsic worth* of music. From the simple song to the complex opera and the time-honoured practice of using music for the celebration of religious services, music has never ceased to accompany the most tender and profound affections of the human mind

and has thus been the indirect means of glorifying
them.

Apart from the existence of an *intrinsic merit*, there
is a second corollary which we wish to emphasize.
Though music possesses beauty of form without any
extrinsic subject, this does not deprive it of the
quality of *individuality*. The act of inventing a
certain theme, and the mode of working it out, are
always so unique and specific as to defy their
inclusion in a wider generality. These processes are
distinctly and unequivocally *individual* in nature. A
theme of Mozart or Beethoven rests on as firm and
independent a foundation as a poem by Goethe, an
epigram by Lessing, a statue by Thorwaldsen, or a
painting by Overbeck. The independent musical
thoughts (themes) possess the identity of a quotation and the distinctness of a painting; they are
individual, personal, eternal.

Unable, as we were, to endorse Hegel's opinion
respecting the want of intellectual merit in music, it
seems to us a still more glaring error on his part to
assert that the sole function of music is the expressing of an "inner non-individuality." Even from
Hegel's musical point of view, which, while over-
looking the inherently form-giving and objective
activity of the composer, conceives music as the free
manifestation of purely *subjective states*, its want of
individuality follows by no means, since the subjec-
tively-producing mind is essentially individual.

How the individuality shows itself in the choice
and working out of the various musical elements, we
have already pointed out in the third chapter. The

*stigma* that music has no subject is, therefore, quite unmerited. Music has a subject—*i.e.*, a musical subject, which is no less a vital spark of the divine fire than the beautiful of any other art. Yet, only by steadfastly denying the existence of any other " subject " in music, is it possible to save its " true subject." The indefinite emotions which at best underlie the other kind of subject, do not explain its spiritual force. The latter can only be attributed to the definite beauty of musical form, as the result of the untrammeled working of the human mind on material susceptible of intellectual manipulation.